RICHARD GIUBERTONI & EMILY C[

SECONDARY SCIENCE IN ACTION

IN ACTION SERIES

A **WALKTHRUs**
PRODUCTION

JOHN CATT
FROM HODDER EDUCATION

To order, please visit www.johncatt.com or contact Customer Service at education@hachette.co.uk / +44 (0)1235 827827.

ISBN: 978 1 9152 6192 2

© Richard Giubertoni and Emily Clark Giubertoni 2024
First published in 2024 by
John Catt from Hodder Education,
An Hachette UK Company
15 Riduna Park, Station Road,
Melton, Woodbridge IP12 1QT
www.johncatt.com

Typeset in the UK.

Cover illustration by Oliver Caviglioli.

Illustrations by DC Graphics and Integra Software Services Pvt. Ltd.

Printed in the UK.

A catalogue record for this title is available from the British Library.

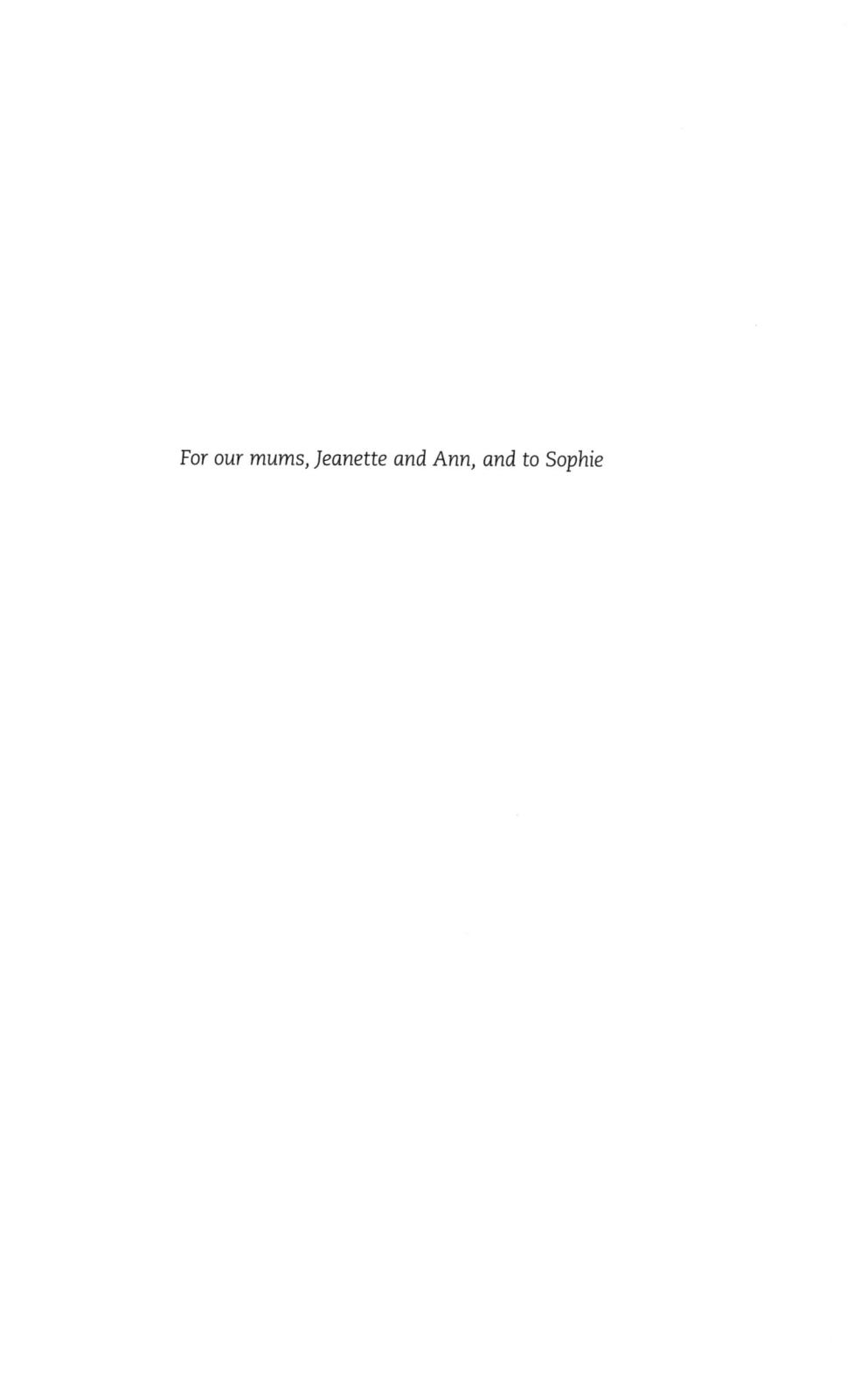

For our mums, Jeanette and Ann, and to Sophie

PRAISE FOR *SECONDARY SCIENCE IN ACTION*

Schools, teachers and teacher trainers have waited a long time for this book. Grounded in the best available evidence on effective science teaching, with practical suggestions for how to apply this knowledge, Emily and Richard's book will make huge a difference to all teachers, whether they are beginning to teach science or are later in their careers.

Dr Richard Churches, Global Head of Research, Education Development Trust and author of *Neuroscience for Teachers* and *Teacher-Led Research*

This book is a must-have for science leaders and teachers! It's invaluable for considering anything from 'big-picture' curriculum and research, to best-practice implementation in your science lab. Wherever science educators are on their journey between expert and novice, there is something useful to be learned from this book.

Katy Micklewright, Head of Early Careers Framework, National Institute of Teaching

This book is an essential guide for every science teacher. Underpinned by a review of the evidence, the authors explain how to embed this research in your science teaching, with practical suggestions and case studies.

Chris Catto, Central Midlands Science Learning Partnership Lead

Practical, comprehensive and anchored in research and evidence, this is a highly valuable resource for all those involved in the delivery of science teaching. The authors use their wide-ranging experience to provide a text that can make a real difference to schools.

Jodh Dhesi, Chief Executive Officer of the King Edward VI Foundation

CONTENTS

ACKNOWLEDGEMENTS

Thank you, Fiza Aslam, Miyah Nicholson, Nasra Jabeen and all the staff at George Perkins Day Nursery for doing such an amazing job looking after Sophie while we were writing this book. She has loved every second, and we couldn't have written the book without knowing she was being cared for with such love and kindness.

Thank you to Sophia Mayor, Head of Science at Bishop Challoner Catholic College, Billy Feenan, Head of Science at Dame Elizabeth Cadbury School, and Jack Perry at Prince Albert High School for offering your subject expertise.

Teaching has been the best job in the world for us both, and so much of that is because we work with incredible people. We would like to acknowledge all the teachers and support staff at Bishop Challoner Catholic College and King Edward VI Aston School for making every work day a good day.

Thank you to Dr Angie Hurd, physics teacher extraordinaire, for being an inspiration every day since we met, and a necessary-for-survival friend every day since July 2008.

Thank you to our editor, Anders, for all you've taught us about the world of publishing.

And finally, thank you Tom Sherrington for having the idea for this book and for trusting us to write it.

The authors and publishers would like to thank the following for permission to reproduce copyright material.

Letter from Albert Einstein © The Hebrew University of Jerusalem. With permission of the Albert Einstein Archives.

Excerpt(s) from THE PERIODIC TABLE by Primo Levi, translated by Raymond Rosenthal, translation copyright © 1984 by Penguin Random House LLC. Used by permission of Schocken Books, an imprint of the Knopf Doubleday Publishing Group, a division of Penguin Random House LLC. All rights reserved.

SERIES FOREWORD

This series of books was commissioned as a WalkThrus Production to complement two of our other series: The *Teaching Walkthrus*, Volumes 1, 2 and 3, and the *In Action* series. We believe that, together, they represent a powerful resource for teachers in schools and colleges in multiple subject settings.

The *In Action* series has proven to be very popular with busy teachers, enabling them to engage with a range of important ideas from cognitive science and from education research more generally. In each book, the authors explore the key ideas from a specific researcher, translating them into practical approaches that teachers can adopt in their practice. So far, the series includes:

- Rosenshine's Principles of Instruction
- Collins et al's Cognitive Apprenticeship
- Fiorella & Mayer's Generative Learning
- Shimamura's MARGE Model of Learning
- Sweller's Cognitive Load Theory
- Wiliam & Leahy's Five Formative Assessment Strategies
- Annie Murphy Paul's The Extended Mind
- Dunlosky's Strengthening the Student Toolbox
- Berger's An Ethic of Excellence
- Bjork & Bjork's Desirable Difficulties
- Ausubel's Meaningful Learning

Each of these books is a guide to interpreting the research in ways that can be applied in real-world classrooms. We have been delighted by the response to the series, with teachers telling us they value the brevity and clarity and the examples of theory in practice. It's so important for teachers to have a good grounding in cognitive science so that they have not only a clear model of how learning happens but also an understanding of all the potential barriers or difficulties that students experience. Bridging the gap between research and practice is a significant challenge because real-world classrooms are so much more complicated than the controlled conditions usually set up to investigate specific concepts in trials. The authors of the *In Action* books are all serving teachers or have taught in schools for many years, so their take on the theories and concepts that their books focus on is important and incredibly useful, grounded in the reality of teaching whole, complex classes.

It's by no means a comprehensive list – not yet – and we recognise that many other aspects of research would benefit from the same treatment. Books on Nuthall's Hidden Lives of Learners, Engelmann's ideas on direct instruction and Bandura's ideas on self-efficacy are all in the pipeline. We would also encourage every teacher to engage with Dan Willingham's *Why Don't Students Like School?*.

Released in parallel with the research-informed *In Action* series, our *Teaching WalkThrus* have also been popular with over 350,000 copies distributed across the three volumes. The idea of breaking ideas down into five-step visual guides, with short punchy descriptions, has proven very successful, allowing teachers to engage with a broad range of ideas in a very accessible format that informs their training, coaching or personal reflection. Significantly, *Teaching WalkThrus* were written in a style that is context free. They are generic in style so that teachers of all subjects in any setting can engage with them, transposing the ideas into their real-world contexts. The 150+ WalkThrus are organised into six main series, each of which represents an important area for professional learning:

Behaviour and relationships

- Lesson management
- Planning for good behaviour
- Positive correction
- Relationships and mindsets

Curriculum planning

- Assessment issues
- Broad design concepts
- Challenge, inclusion, diversity
- Detailed planning

Explaining and modelling

- Giving explanations and modelling
- Reading and writing
- Standards, expectations and scaffolding

- Types of explanations

Questioning and feedback
- Assessment
- Core questioning techniques
- Deeper questioning techniques
- Feedback

Practice and retrieval
- Guided to independent practice
- Reading
- Building fluency
- Retrieval practice
- Support and challenge

Mode B teaching
- Choices and creativity
- Making it real
- Oracy
- Student directed activities

With over 4000 schools having engaged with our online WalkThrus toolkit, we know that a great deal of valuable professional learning can be supported with our generic guides as a starting point. However, throughout each book we are at pains to stress the crucial need to adapt the ideas for specific circumstances. A five-step visual WalkThrus guide is not a set of rigid rules – it is a framework for thinking through an idea, deconstructing it so that teachers can then reconstruct it themselves, forming their own mental models for enacting powerful techniques in their own classrooms. That's the spirit.

Now, having explored research ideas in the *In Action* series and general pedagogical ideas in WalkThrus, we felt that the logical next step was to bring in subject-specific books in this new series, completing the third pillar of the trio: research, pedagogy, curriculum. Each book in the *In Action* subject series has been written by practising teachers who were tasked with presenting a summary of important ideas and debates from their subject to support busy teachers in their work. We have not imposed a rigid common format and our authors were encouraged to share their own perspectives with our readers. There is no definitive book on teaching science or history or maths or physical education – so these books are explicitly written with that in mind. The books represent the authors' personal perspective on how the ideas that circulate within each subject community can translate into great practice in the classroom. Once again, we invite readers to then adapt and adopt the ideas that make sense in their context.

I have to congratulate each author on their excellent work. It's daunting to summarise and capture the spirit of a subject, balancing depth of detail with sufficient breadth of coverage of content and related debates and implementation issues – all in what is meant to be a short book. If there is one thing that characterises all our books it is that they are accessible to teachers who are time poor. Each book in this series achieves that goal – they have an energy to them and a brilliant balance of rigour, steeped in experience with teaching the subject, alongside tons of examples to bring things to life.

We hope you find this book interesting and useful, adding an important dimension to your wider reading as a teacher doing the most important work there is: developing young people so that they have the knowledge, experience, confidence and wisdom they need to make sense of their world and play their part in the communities they belong to.

ABOUT THE AUTHORS

Emily Clark Giubertoni has been an English teacher in mainstream schools in Birmingham since 2008. She is currently SCITT Director, and Dean of Bishop Challoner Training School Alliance. She leads professional growth, Initial Teacher Training, Early Career Teacher development, and leadership training for schools and teachers across the West Midlands. She has spoken at conferences and published articles on professional growth and women in leadership.

Richard Giubertoni has been a Chemistry teacher in secondary schools in Walsall, Reading and Birmingham since 2008, and head of Chemistry since 2012. He is currently the school Lead for Evidence Informed Education at King Edward VI Aston School, where his research interests include the use of digital technologies, metacognition, and stretching the most able learners.

CHAPTER 1
WHAT IS TEACHING SCIENCE ALL ABOUT?

Why do we teach science?

Science can inspire awe in the world around us and, as the Education Endowment Foundation (EEF, 2018) report on improving secondary science tells us, 'Every secondary teacher knows the deep satisfaction that comes from lighting the fires of interest in young people'. Building this curiosity allows students to explore and understand the beauty and complexity of the Universe, from the microscopic to the cosmic. This curiosity can be leveraged by teachers and by the students themselves to create lifelong learners who are keen to explore and gain knowledge.

Science teaching is about inspiring young people with a fundamental understanding of the world around us. Science teaching should aim to teach students to recognise the power of science and, in so doing, ignite an enthusiasm for a subject that might take them in many different directions of study and work.

An understanding of science, its procedures, its explanations and its methods helps students to think critically about the world around them. Another aim of science teaching is to give students a degree of scientific literacy, enabling them to make informed choices in their personal lives and as part of a democratic society.

Studying science helps students develop critical-thinking skills, analytical reasoning and problem-solving abilities. An understanding of the scientific method allows students to analyse data and to draw logical conclusions. These skills give students options moving forward, in the world of further study, the world of work and in engaging with society. Science is a key subject for various fields of medicine, engineering and technology. By studying science, students are equipped for higher education and their future careers.

Science helps students comprehend and address major global challenges such as climate change, global pandemics and other health-related issues. Educating students about these topics prepares them to become responsible and informed citizens who can engage fully with the debates of the contemporary world.

What do we want students to get from studying science?

A student coming to a science classroom should expect to get more than a list of facts. A student walking away from a year studying science should expect to be given a whole range of intellectual gifts:

- understanding of the disciplinary knowledge of science (how to work and think like a scientist)
- understanding of global issues from a scientific perspective and the ability to develop their own opinions on these issues
- aspiration to work in science, technology, engineering and maths subjects (STEM) and an understanding of the vast range of STEM-related careers open to a student, post-GCSE and beyond
- aspiration to study science in higher education
- understanding of the diversity of science as a field, both historically and currently
- understanding of the value of science and the work of scientists.

If we can give our students these things, we have done well as teachers. We will fulfil the wider purpose of teachers in preparing students to be empowered in their own future paths, and to be active and informed members of society.

What are the big-picture questions about science?

Thinking like a scientist is a mindset that goes beyond the individual facts of each subject discipline. Science teachers are responsible, not just for teaching the subject content, but also for instilling a way of thinking about the world. Harlen (2015) summarised four big ideas in science that underpin all of science teaching:

1 Science is about finding the cause or causes of phenomena in the natural world.

2 Scientific explanations, theories and models are those that best fit the evidence available at a particular time.

3 The knowledge produced by science is used in engineering and technologies to create products to serve human ends.

4 Applications of science often have ethical, social, economic and political implications.

Why is it important for science teachers to understand these principles? In teaching, it is easy to get lost in the minutiae of a single lesson, to focus on how well students have done in the five recap questions in the starter, or to be wholly in the moment ensuring the safety of students using Bunsen burners for the first time. Individual lessons are obviously crucial to student learning, but unless teachers step back occasionally to acknowledge the bigger picture and the end goal, an individual lesson can drift into meaninglessness.

It took Seurat 18 months to paint A *Sunday Afternoon on the Island of La Grande Jatte*. For months, he worked on preliminary details and sketches. When painting, he focused on tiny details of the grass and the clothing. He worked in pointillism, crafting the painting using tiny dots. Close up, the dots and the colours might be beautiful, but it is only in stepping back and looking at the big picture that the beauty of the whole painting becomes apparent. Putting the dots together to make a small square of grass means nothing without the big-picture concept it is building towards. In the same way, occasionally science teachers need to take a step back and look at the big picture. Yes, the lesson has gone well, but how does it help students understand these big questions about the world? How has it achieved the goals of science teaching as a discipline? These questions should be fundamental to science teaching.

How much time should science take?

How much time is enough? Particularly at GCSE, science teaching can feel squeezed. The Ofsted Science Research Review (2021) found that in the UK, 'evidence from analysis of school timetables in England suggests that insufficient time is often allocated to teach Triple science ... This means that some schools restrict Triple science to just high-attaining pupils who are presumed to be able to cope with the more intensive timetable.' Triple science students study three separate sciences *but* also in more depth and with extra topics, obtaining three separate GCSEs at the end of their study. In contrast, Combined science or Double science is a qualification in which the teaching of all three sciences is combined, taught at a lower level, and students are rewarded with two science GCSEs.

This becomes problematic when there are students who are desperate (or even just keen) to study separate sciences to a higher level but who are denied the opportunity due to class sizes and timetable demands. When not enough time is allocated, students who could otherwise do well might have their potential limited. Exam boards suggest that a double award qualification should be assigned 240 teaching hours, or approximately 3 hours a week based on 39 teaching weeks over 2 years. In comparison, each science GCSE when studied as a Triple award requires 120 hours, resulting in 1.5 hours a week per science or a total of 4.5 hours of science teaching a week.

In the real world, timetable and class limits exist. Even within a curriculum designed to fit the timetable, it can still feel like there is too much to cover or not enough time to cover it well. Luckily, the EEF research report 'Improving Secondary Science' (2018) makes a succinct but powerful point:

> 'Evidence-informed science teaching is not about fitting more into a tight timetable: it's about using limited time and resources as smartly as possible, by focusing on what is most likely to have a positive impact.'

This book is about the smartest ways to teach science; for example, how we can teach science:

- with rigorous intellectual standards
- quickly and efficiently
- in an intelligent manner, maximising opportunities and allowing for the unique limits of individual schools
- while working independently, using teacher autonomy to provide the best science education possible for our students.

Further reading

Education Endowment Foundation (2018) *Improving Secondary Science: Guidance report.* Available at: https://educationendowmentfoundation.org.uk/education-evidence/guidance-reports/science-ks3-ks4

Harlen, W. (ed.) (2015) *Working with Big Ideas of Science Education.* IAP. Available at: https://www.ase.org.uk/bigideas

The Ofsted Science Research Review (2021) *Research review series: science* https://www.gov.uk/government/publications/research-review-series-science/research-review-series-science#introduction

CHAPTER 2
WHAT DOES THE RESEARCH TELL US ABOUT TEACHING SECONDARY SCIENCE?

This book is informed by contemporary research about teaching secondary science. In this chapter you will find brief synopses of some important texts for science teachers. Reading these in full will be a valuable exercise, but as a starting point, here you will find summaries of the key points from each text to give an insight into the core ideas explored elsewhere in this book.

Improving Secondary Science: Seven recommendations for improving science in secondary schools (2018)

What kind of research is it?

This guidance report published by the EEF brings together research into seven practical, evidence-based strategies for effective science teaching. Each of the seven recommendations is supported by an evidence summary, examples from practice and further reading.

What does it say?

1 Preconceptions: build on the ideas that pupils bring to lessons.

2 Self-regulation: help pupils direct their own learning.

3 Modelling: use models to support understanding.

4 Memory: support pupils to retain and retrieve knowledge.

5 Practical work: use practical work purposefully and as part of a learning sequence.

6 Language of science: develop scientific vocabulary and support pupils to read and write about science.

7 Feedback: use structured feedback to develop pupils' thinking.

How can it help me in my own teaching?

This is an excellent document for reflecting on different elements of basic classroom practice. Each recommendation is something that should be routinely used in strong, everyday classroom practice. By reading the strategies and reflecting on their own practice, science teachers can evaluate and improve their classroom practice with ease.

Where can I read it?

Read the full report online, here: https://educationendowmentfoundation.org.uk/education-evidence/guidance-reports/science-ks3-ks4

Ofsted Research review series: science (2021)

What kind of research is it?

Published by Ofsted, this is a literature review of the research underpinning effective science teaching. Among other things, it explores the literature on curriculum progression, pedagogy and assessment in science.

What does it say?

The detailed literature review concludes by summarising three core principles of science teaching today:

1   A high-quality science education is rooted in an authentic understanding of what science is.

2   A high-quality science curriculum prioritises pupils building knowledge of key concepts in a meaningful way that reflects how knowledge is organised in the scientific disciplines.

3   This means that science curriculums should be planned to take account of the function of knowledge in relation to future learning.

How can it help me in my own teaching?

This is a very detailed literature review – including 258 referencing footnotes – which serves as a helpful summary of the research, so saving a busy teacher from having to read a large volume of primary sources.

Let's look at some of the key takeaways in action.

Curriculum planning

An effective science curriculum is structured to build learning over time. Pupils should be taught how concepts are related so that, as they progress through the science curriculum, new knowledge gets systematically integrated into pre-existing knowledge. This enables synthesis of larger concepts, allowing pupils to operate at abstract levels.

Chunking of knowledge should be used, allowing pupils to successfully build knowledge of science concepts and their relationships over multiple years, without working memory overload.

Both substantive and disciplinary knowledge are important, and they should be taught in an integrated way; the school curriculum should be organised so that disciplinary knowledge is embedded within the substantive content of biology, chemistry and physics.

Teaching about rates of reaction in chemistry presents a good opportunity for students to develop both substantive and disciplinary knowledge. The curriculum sequencing and chunking of this topic should be designed carefully to support students in learning how rates of reaction are affected by different conditions.

By first exploring the theory of how chemical reactions happen – the ideas of collision theory, activation energy and successful collisions – students will learn the substantive knowledge that a successful collision is one that has energy greater than or equal to the activation energy of that reaction, and that the rate of reaction is determined by the number of successful collisions per second. Armed with this knowledge, students can now predict what will happen when conditions change and they can start to design experiments to test and measure changing rates. In these experiments, disciplinary skills of how to measure, how to control variables and how to analyse data can be taught. In the analysis stage, graphing skills can be taught, including how to find the gradient of a curve at a certain point using a tangent.

Building knowledge of scientific concepts

Revisiting key topics should not involve simple repetition, but rather should be an opportunity for new knowledge to be added to the developing 'big concept' being studied.

The idea that all matter is made up of small particles is one that develops throughout a student's learning journey in science. At secondary level, students would normally start by learning about solids, liquids and gases, and how the particles – represented by spheres – are arranged. This is later revisited when students learn about elements, mixtures and compounds by looking at these particles in more detail. From here, understanding builds in several ways, as students are taught what atoms are made of, how atoms link together in different ways and how these factors give rise to different bulk properties. By revisiting and building on the initial idea, students form a deep understanding of the big idea.

Disciplinary knowledge

Once disciplinary knowledge is introduced, it should be practised across different topics and subjects. This allows pupils to learn how the same disciplinary knowledge is used in different substantive contexts.

One of the key areas of disciplinary knowledge that students are expected to master through their science curriculum is data analysis, especially how to process and present scientific data to identify trends and patterns. This normally takes the form of presenting data from practical work in tables and graphs.

For a student to master this skill, they must be able to take data from a practical and present it using the most appropriate type of graph. Students should be taught specifically how to lay out a graph – putting the independent variable on the x-axis and the dependent variable on the y-axis, and understanding that the independent variable is the one they controlled and changed, whereas the dependent variable is the outcome of the experiment. Different types of graph, such as bar charts, histograms and line graphs, should be taught and the contexts in which scientists use these graphs explained.

Once students understand these basics, data analysis using graphs should be revisited as an integral part of any practical activity that collects quantitative data. In this way, the disciplinary knowledge is applied in different topics.

Questions can be used to guide students into choosing the right kind of graph for their data:

1 What is the independent variable?

2 What is the dependent variable?

3 What variable goes on the x-axis? What is its unit?

4 What variable goes on the y-axis? What is its unit?

5 Is the data discrete or continuous?

6 What kind of graph is suitable for this data?

7 What are the reasons for choosing this kind of graph for the data?

These questions should scaffold the task of drawing a graph and can be applied to any practical that collects data. As students gain a greater level of mastery in this disciplinary area, these questions can – and should – be reduced or removed.

RADAAR

Curriculum plans should predict misconceptions and plan to address them. Planning a curriculum that develops in small steps will minimise the chances of misconceptions developing. The EEF suggests the use of the RADAAR (research, anticipate, diagnose, address, assess and review) planning framework to enable teachers to predict and plan for misconceptions in a strategic way.

Research

In the research stage, the teacher uses their knowledge of how pupils learn the subject to identify potential and likely misconceptions. For example, a common misconception held by students when learning about forces is that acceleration is always in the direction in which an object is travelling (rather than in the direction of the change of velocity of the object).

Anticipate

Using the questions below, the teacher can plan for this misconception and develop strategies for dealing with it in the classroom:

1 What are the prerequisite ideas needed to access the topic?

Students need to know what a force is, defining it as a push or a pull. They need to know that forces have a magnitude (how strong they are) and a direction (making them a vector quantity).

2 What is the common misconception in this topic?

Acceleration always acts in the direction of travel of an object.

3 What is the key vocabulary for this topic?

Force, acceleration, balanced, unbalanced, magnitude.

4 Are there any potentially confusing words or terms that could be avoided, for example, words that have a non-scientific meaning?

The use of the term 'deceleration' can be confusing for some students as it reinforces the idea that acceleration is in the direction of travel and that deceleration is against it.

5 Are there any terms that you need to be particularly careful about using as they are commonly misused?

'Acceleration' is confused with the direction of travel.

6 How will you explicitly link to and activate prior knowledge?

Ask students to draw diagrams showing the forces acting on objects in different situations. This will remind students of how forces act on objects.

By asking themselves these questions in the 'anticipate' stage, teachers can identify common misconceptions, the vocabulary and language needed and the prerequisite knowledge required for a topic, and include these elements in their curriculum plan. This should give them a strong idea of the key misconceptions and a plan for how to address them.

Diagnose and address
In this stage, the teacher moves into the classroom environment. They use a hinge question to diagnose whether the likely misconception they have identified exists in this specific class, and then address it if needed.

For example, the teacher could display a force diagram of an object with unbalanced forces and clearly in motion, for example, a car slowing down while driving down a road. They would ask students to draw an arrow showing the direction of the acceleration.

1 If a student's arrow is in the direction of movement, they have the misconception that acceleration is always in the direction of travel.

2 If a student's arrow opposes the direction in which the car is moving, they understand that acceleration is the change in speed.

3 If a student draws an arrow going in any other direction, further misconceptions have been exposed.

If student misconceptions are exposed, the teacher can use a demonstration, explicit teaching and examples to clarify the idea.

Assess and review
Finally, the teacher should continue to pose questions with different contexts and wording to check that student learning is firmly embedded. Teacher explanations are crucial. Discovery-based learning has been debunked; pupils should not be expected to arrive at scientific explanations by themselves without sufficient prior knowledge.

Plan for science-specific literacy and numeracy development
Subject leaders and teachers of mathematics and science should work together to understand how and when knowledge taught in their respective subjects is similar and different.

The ability to measure the gradient of a curved line is a higher-level graph-analysis skill for students. It has applications in several topics: calculating rates of reactions in chemistry and rates of biological processes, and acceleration in physics. The skill of drawing a tangent to the curved line using a ruler and measuring the gradient of this tangent will be taught in mathematics lessons, as well as in science lessons. Maths and science teachers should work together to make sure this skill is taught in the same way to reinforce learning.

Pupils should be explicitly taught to read, write and speak like scientists. Every teacher is a teacher of literacy. Teaching students specific scientific literacy skills should be part of every science teacher's routine practice.

Identify the literacy skill you want to teach. Teach students to read, write and speak like scientists using the same explicit steps you use to teach scientific knowledge: break it down for your students, model what it should look like, give opportunities for them to practise and provide feedback on their work. Give students success criteria to support them with the literacy skills being practised, not just to measure their substantive knowledge.

Scientific vocabulary

Explicit vocabulary teaching from early years onwards is crucial for successful science teaching; exposure to high-quality reading materials, which include scientific vocabulary in context, is a key strategy.

Beck, McKeown and Kucan (2013) sort vocabulary into three tiers of utility:

- **Tier 1** – words used in everyday conversations

- **Tier 2** – ambitious vocabulary that students might encounter in different contexts; it is important to teach the scientific-specific meaning of these words

- **Tier 3** – subject-specific vocabulary that is integral to the subject.

In each lesson, identify the Tier 2 and Tier 3 vocabulary you can teach. The table on the following page gives some examples. →

Tier 2	Tier 3
• analyse	• homeostasis
• evaluate	• endothermic
• hypothesise	• catalyst
• argument	• reactant

To teach vocabulary, the following strategies can be helpful:

- Talk about the word and co-construct a 'class definition'.

- Break down the word into parts and identify the roots of the word, which might give clues to the meaning. For example, the Greek suffix '–thermic', meaning 'to heat', gives a clue about the definitions of the words 'exothermic', 'endothermic' and 'hypothermic'.

- Show the word in two sentences, one demonstrating correct usage and the other incorrect. Ask students to identify the correct usage (and explain why the incorrect usage is wrong).

- Reward students for using Tier 2 and Tier 3 scientific vocabulary correctly.

Have a clear rationale for why you are doing practicals

Practical work should be planned with clear substantive and disciplinary objectives. Inspiring awe and wonder is a legitimate outcome of practical work.

When planning a practical, map out the substantive and disciplinary learning outcomes you want to achieve. Let's go through this process for a practical to investigate the reactivity of Group 7 elements: carrying out a set of displacement reactions by reacting the elements dissolved in water with solutions of salts containing these elements.

Substantive knowledge objectives:

- to know the order of reactivity of the halogen elements in the practical

- to know that a more reactive element displaces a less reactive element from solution.   →

> Disciplinary knowledge objectives:
>
> • to be able to identify when a chemical reaction has taken place
>
> • to be able to make predictions about the reactivity of other elements in the group based on data.

Assessment in science classrooms

Assessment in the science classroom has three core purposes:

1 to frequently check pupils' understanding, to identify gaps and misconceptions, following up with subject-specific feedback to enable pupils to make progress

2 to prevent pupils from forgetting what they have learned via the testing effect, which suggests that regular, low-stakes retrieval tests have benefits for increasing long-term memory

3 summative assessment to check that pupils have met their goals.

Avoid overuse of exam-board-generated materials for assessment as this can inadvertently narrow the curriculum. Moderation should be used to make sure teacher assessment is accurate.

Use carefully selected resources

High-quality textbooks should be used as an important resource for learning and teaching science. These might be complemented by online materials, although care should be taken to ensure the curriculum still has coherence if resources from multiple sources are used.

School leaders should strategically reflect on the use of resources and staff to enable the best science education:

■ Ensure teachers and technicians have access to high-quality, subject-specific continuing professional development (CPD). Professional bodies and STEM Learning are good sources.

■ Plan the timetable to maximise teaching in specialisms and duplicating the teaching of year groups or key stages for newer teachers.

■ Allocate enough time to teach the planned curriculum.

Where can I read it?

You can read the full report online, here: https://www.gov.uk/government/publications/research-review-series-science/research-review-series-science

Good Practical Science (2017)

What kind of research is it?

This report, published by the Gatsby Foundation, is based on evidence from six countries with a successful track record of science education and on surveys with experts from 19 countries. Based on this data, the writers of the report drafted 10 benchmarks for effective practical science, that can be used as a self-evaluation tool by schools, teachers and technicians

What does it say?

The report offers 10 benchmarks that are features of effective practical science. In the full report, each benchmark is supported by a summary and set of criteria statements.

1 Planned practical science

2 Purposeful practical science

3 Expert teachers

4 Frequent and varied practical science

5 The laboratory facilities and equipment

6 Technical support

7 Real experiments, virtual enhancements

8 Investigative projects

9 A balanced approach to risk

10 Assessment fit for purpose

How can it help me in my own teaching?

Science is a practical subject. The best CPD for teachers is usually subject specific. This report can be used by science teachers as part of their CPD, either through personal reflection, mentoring and coaching, or departmental discussions about improving practice.

Putting the Gatsby benchmarks into practice

At Bishop Challoner Catholic College, we believe practicals should complement the science curriculum, providing enriching opportunities to develop skills and enhance knowledge. Across the key stages, practicals are embedded into the curriculum, with schemes of work that specify our intent in delivering practicals as well as linking them to career opportunities. We have a team of technicians who lead on their specialism, advising the teachers on the range and delivery of practicals. We seek out continued CPD, both externally and internally, in our department meetings. Our department training is led by expert teachers; staff and technicians share and review best practice about the effective delivery of practicals.

The student experience is of frequent exposure to practicals, and end-of-topic assessments have a section for practical skills to be assessed. Through using a variety of equipment in the laboratories, the students develop their disciplinary skills alongside their substantive knowledge of the topic. Students use technology in science by using virtual reality headsets to simulate the inside of a cell or an atom, as well as using their electrical kits. Through a science club and STEM projects running throughout the Key Stage 3 curriculum, the students have opportunities to plan, investigate, design and evaluate practical work. We have an enrichment programme of trips, including to London's Science Museum, the National Space Centre in Leicester and crime scene investigation days. These allow the students to see further applications of practical work to careers, as well as inspiring their love of science.

Sophia Mayor, Head of Science, Bishop Challoner Catholic College, Birmingham

Where can I read it?

Read the full report online, here: https://www.gatsby.org.uk/education/programmes/support-for-practical-science-in-schools

Working with Big Ideas of Science Education (2015)

What kind of research is it?

This is a report from an international seminar of science experts, focused on identifying the big ideas that should underpin an effective science curriculum to enable students to 'understand, enjoy and marvel at the natural world'.

What does it say?

The report identifies 10 big ideas *of* science and four big ideas *about* science that all students should have the opportunity to learn before the end of compulsory education. Each principle is described in some detail – what it means and how it should be understood – as well as being contextualised within different conceptions of progression.

Ten big ideas of science

1 All matter in the Universe is made of very small particles.

2 Objects can affect other objects at a distance.

3 Changing the movement of an object requires a net force to be acting on it.

4 The total amount of energy in the Universe is always the same but can be transferred from one energy store to another during an event.

5 The composition of the Earth and its atmosphere and the processes occurring within them shape the Earth's surface and its climate.

6 Our Solar System is a very small part of one of billions of galaxies in the Universe.

7 Organisms are organised on a cellular basis and have a finite lifespan.

8 Organisms require a supply of energy and materials for which they often depend on, or compete with, other organisms.

9 Genetic information is passed down from one generation of organisms to another.

10 The diversity of organisms, living and extinct, is the result of evolution.

Four big ideas about science

1 Science is about finding the cause or causes of phenomena in the natural world.

2 Scientific explanations, theories and models are those that best fit the evidence available at a particular time.

3 The knowledge produced by science is used in engineering and technologies to create products to serve human ends.

4 Applications of science often have ethical, social, economic and political implications.

The report includes a very helpful overview for each of the big ideas, specifying exactly what subject content is involved from age 5 all the way to age 17. Pages 20–33 are a brilliant resource for developing teacher understanding and expertise in curriculum progression in a specifically scientific context. The report further explores effective practice in pedagogy, content and assessment, again offering practical suggestions to science teachers at all levels.

How can it help me in my own teaching?

It is a superb resource for developing teacher expertise in curriculum progression in a specifically scientific context. Here are four ways you could use the big ideas in your own planning and teaching:

1 Use it to review your curriculum overview. Are all the big ideas covered?

2 Use it to review your curriculum plan for developing learning over time. Pick one of the big ideas and track the opportunities for students to engage with it from Year 7 to Year 11 or 13. Does your curriculum have a coherent approach to building understanding of this theme over time?

3 Share the big ideas with students so that they can see how individual lessons contribute to developing an understanding of them.

4 Promote the way the big ideas exist beyond the classroom, in the work of scientists, politicians and those working in industry today. A display board on the four big ideas about science will help students see the real-world applications of their lessons.

Where can I read it?

Read the full report online, here: https://www.ase.org.uk/bigideas

How do I stay up to date with developments in research around science teaching?

Make sure you are signed up for membership of the professional associations for science teaching: the Royal Society of Chemistry; the Institute of Physics; the Royal Society of Biology; and the Association of Science Education.

Sign up for alerts for when Ofsted releases new research related to science: https://www.gov.uk/government/collections/ofsted-schools-survey-reports#science

Sign up for newsletters from the EEF to get notifications about the latest research reports, including science: https://educationendowmentfoundation.org.uk/sign-up

Further reading

Beck, I., McKeown, M., and Kucan, L. (2013, 2nd ed.) *Bringing Words to Life: Robust vocabulary instruction.* New York: Guilford Press.

CHAPTER 3
HOW DO I DEVELOP DIFFERENT SCIENTIFIC SKILLS IN MY STUDENTS?

Developing student expertise in science requires mastery of two fields: substantive knowledge and disciplinary knowledge.

Substantive knowledge: How do I teach students the key facts in science?

Substantive knowledge, at its simplest level, can be understood as the *facts* that students must learn. This includes the different theories, concepts and models in biology, physics and chemistry. In the National Curriculum in England, the substantive knowledge students are expected to learn can be found under the heading 'Subject content'. Substantive knowledge includes a wide spectrum of content from comparatively straightforward single facts (e.g. electric current is measured in amperes) to understanding the big ideas in a subject (e.g. the concept of a field as key to analysing electrical effects).

Why is substantive knowledge important to teach in science?

For a student to progress, they must move from being a novice to an expert scientist. The key difference between an expert and a novice is their level and organisation of science-specific knowledge. The more substantive knowledge a student has, the easier it is for them to make sense of unfamiliar material by linking it to existing schemas.

A KS4 student learning about the difference between eukaryotic and prokaryotic cells, and the main sub-cellular structures contained within, would rely heavily on their understanding of the basic cell structures from KS3. If the student already understands that all cells contain a nucleus and cytoplasm, and that plant cells have significantly different adaptations from those found in animal cells, it is far easier for them to understand that cells contain additional organelles with specific functions and roles. →

In chemistry, when students are learning about structure and bonding at KS4, a strong understanding of the particle model from KS3 is an essential foundation. This will help students to grasp why some structures tend to be gases (molecular covalent bonding) and why others tend to be solids (ionic, macromolecular and metallic bonding). A student with a strong knowledge of the particle model can relate the new structures to their current knowledge of bonding and then can easily build on this model by adding ideas about why particular structures tend to be gases or solids.

What strategies work well in science to teach substantive knowledge?

Substantive knowledge grows over time as students layer new learning onto prior knowledge. Fundamental concepts in each science discipline, such as the conservation of energy or the particle model, are taught again and again, each time adding new facts, concepts and ideas to student understanding. For this to work well, teachers must have a good understanding of the curriculum across the ages and phases they teach, so they can confidently make links forwards and backwards.

New knowledge must be explicitly taught by the teacher, giving the students the facts, ideas and explanations that they need to build their knowledge. Explicit instruction from the teacher minimises the chances of misconceptions and helps students build connections between knowledge.

Consider the example of cell organelle function in KS4 biology. The teacher should describe these organelles and what they do within the cell. Explicit instruction can take a variety of forms: teacher explanation, worked examples and student reading. Students should not be expected to somehow try and discover the function of these organelles by themselves. If given a picture of a ribosome, it is extremely unlikely that a student could intuit its true function – reading mRNA and using it to build proteins out of amino acids – from their pre-existing knowledge of cells.

Retrieval practice and low-stakes tests

Once it has been taught, substantive knowledge must be firmly fixed into the student's long-term memory and linked effectively to both previous and future learning.

Evidence suggests that teachers should rely heavily on retrieval practice and low-stakes testing. Retrieval practice often takes place at the start of a lesson, to reactivate knowledge that will be relevant to the lesson. This approach is known as 'priming'. Questions are designed to prime students for the subject content in the lesson by asking them to recall the specific prior knowledge that underpins that new learning.

So, a lesson about cell organelles in KS4 would start with a short, low-stakes test asking students to recall the key ideas from KS3 about cell structure and function that will be required for an understanding of the lesson about to be taught. For example:

1 Name a part of a cell that both plant and animal cells have.

2 Name a part of a cell that plant cells have, but not animal cells.

3 What is the function of the nucleus in an animal cell?

4 Which part of a plant cell uses sunlight to make energy stores?

5 Where in a plant cell is the vacuole found?

6 Where are the instructions for a cell found?

At the end of the lesson (or part way through it) more low-stakes testing can be used. This should seek to blend the pre-existing KS3 knowledge with that being taught during the current lesson. For example:

1 Where in a cell can a ribosome be found?

2 Which types of cells (animal, plant, bacterial or algal) have a cell wall?

3 In plant cells, what is the cell wall made from?

4 Which types of cells (animal, plant, bacterial or algal) contain chloroplasts?

5 What is the function of a ribosome?

6 Where in the cell do the instructions interpreted by the ribosomes come from?

What pitfalls should you avoid when teaching substantive knowledge?

A major pitfall when teaching substantive knowledge is focusing on covering and memorising subject content while ignoring the importance of disciplinary knowledge. Students who are taught a science curriculum that focuses only on mastering substantive knowledge are at risk of learning misconceptions. Reducing science lessons to a list of 'facts to be learned' affects student motivation and interest in the subject, by robbing it of the challenge, problem-solving opportunities and real-world applications that make it engaging.

Finally, ignoring the disciplinary knowledge of science disempowers students from understanding science in the real world. Centuries ago, the geocentric model of the Solar System placed the Earth at the centre: this explanation of the Solar System would have been taught as accepted fact. Today, this model has been disproved, and we teach a heliocentric model, placing the Sun at the centre of the Solar System. If we simply teach students the heliocentric model, we can be sure they will answer examination questions with a reasonable degree of success. However, if we teach them how the current model came into being and how the geocentric model was disproved, we are also teaching our students how science evolves.

Even current ideas and explanations could be proved wrong in the future! Scientists are always looking at evidence and trying to find the best explanations. Scientists don't just accept what they are told on authority. In a world where scientific controversies dominate headlines, from *in vitro* fertilisation to Covid and vaccines, it is more important than ever to teach students to understand the how and why behind the knowledge which science presents as 'substantive'.

Disciplinary knowledge: How do I teach students to understand scientific method?

Disciplinary knowledge can be understood as knowledge of the scientific method, working scientifically or understanding how scientists make discoveries and develop scientific explanations. It includes the processes scientists use to establish the knowledge that we then teach as substantive knowledge.

In the National Curriculum, disciplinary knowledge for each key stage is set out under the heading 'Working scientifically'. Disciplinary knowledge is more than just 'doing practicals' and it is a major misconception to reduce it to a set of simple skills.

To develop strong disciplinary knowledge, students must be taught:

- scientific methods for answering questions, including experimentation, categorisation, modelling, synthesis and pattern identification

- knowledge of apparatus and measurement techniques
- scientific data-analysis methods
- scientific analysis, evaluation and explanations
- scientific thinking, including development of scientific method over time and current issues in science.

Why is disciplinary knowledge important to teaching science?

Without an understanding of scientific disciplinary knowledge, students risk seeing science as a list of facts about the world that have arisen, fully formed, from the mind of enlightened individuals. This idea misses the essence of the scientific method – that theories and ideas arise from evidence – and most crucially that these theories are not above questioning if new evidence arises that contradicts them. It is, therefore, essential that disciplinary knowledge is taught effectively.

For those students who go on to work in the field of STEM, an understanding of how scientists work will be crucial to their success in higher education and the workplace. All students will experience times in their lives when an understanding of the scientific method and how scientists work helps them to make personal, social and economic decisions. When the Covid-19 vaccine was released, the concept of vaccine hesitancy hit the news. Misinformation about the vaccine and its effects spread through social media, and for those without a basic understanding of the work of scientists and their interplay with government, unscientific and potentially dangerous information seemed trustworthy. In this case, a wider spread understanding of the way that scientists develop vaccines might have helped reduce public fear and anxiety, and could potentially have encouraged increased uptake of the vaccine.

An understanding of the basic questions scientists ask is crucial for empowering all students to engage with socio-scientific issues as they are presented through news and social media. In Ben Goldacre's blog *Bad Science* (2008), he deconstructs a news report claiming that a scientific study had found that living close to mobile phone masts was a cause of suicide. These findings would be very worrying to the uninformed reader, but they can also be easily debunked by asking some simple disciplinary questions:

- What data were the findings based on?
- What is meant by 'average distance'?
- Was a control group used?

- What qualifications, authority and expertise does the researcher hold to give their findings weight?

In the phone-mast case, there were no convincing answers to any of these questions: disciplinary knowledge enabled Goldacre to disprove the headline and go on with his life unbothered by proximity to mobile phone masts.

What strategies work well in science to teach disciplinary knowledge?

Disciplinary knowledge needs to be taught explicitly. In some ways, the strategies should, therefore, be the same as those for substantive knowledge.

High-quality explanations

Use the following checklist to help you evaluate the quality of your explanations of disciplinary knowledge:

- Have you explained the scientific terminology in use? (Don't assume students understand it.)

- Have you given lots of examples?

- Have you told the story? Storytelling helps us remember explanations more effectively. Is there a famous scientist or anecdote you can link to the concept? Narrative examples will help students remember.

- Have you given a negative example, telling students what *not* to do and why?

- Have you continually checked that students are following your explanation?

Retrieval practice tasks and low-stakes testing

Just as with substantive knowledge, students can be tested on disciplinary knowledge through recap quizzes, 'Do Nows' or low-stakes tests. Questions could be designed to refresh the knowledge needed for the current lesson, or to rehearse learning from a previous week or term, building long-term memories of key information.

For example, the questions on the next page could be used as a retrieval practice task to recap student learning from a previous lesson on the skills of graph drawing, and describing trends and patterns in data. You could also use the scenario at the start of a lesson on describing data in graphical format, using the questions as a primer to help students think about what the graph shows, before exposing them to other graphs and sets of data showing different relationships.

In chemistry, the reaction between magnesium and hydrochloric acid was looked at in an experiment. A mass of powdered magnesium was added to 10 cm³ of hydrochloric acid and the resulting temperature change in the solution was measured. The results were used to produce the graph in Figure 1.

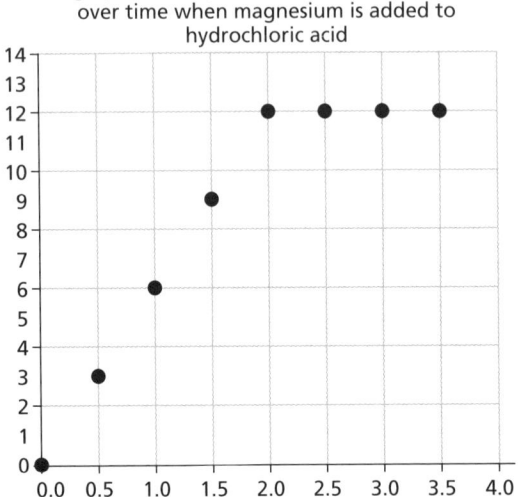

A graph showing the change in temperature over time when magnesium is added to hydrochloric acid

▲ **Figure 1 Temperature change when magnesium is added to hydrochloric acid**

1 What is missing from this graph?

2 What kind of variable is the mass of magnesium?

3 Why is it important to control some variables in this experiment?

4 Name a control variable for this experiment.

5 Describe the trend in results from 0 g to 2 g of magnesium added.

6 Why do you think the trend in results changes after 2 g of magnesium have been added?

Reading

Find articles that explore the work of scientists, scientific research or the history of the scientific process. Read these with the students, or set them as homework. Articles can be easily adapted for the reading age of your students by copying the article into ChatGPT and using the prompt 'adapt this article for a reading age of 12 keeping all scientific vocabulary'. Remember to read through and check the resulting article.

Give your students a glossary to help them understand specific scientific vocabulary and devise key reading questions using *who, what, when, where, why* and *how* prompts to help them deconstruct the texts.

Here are a few useful links to get you started:

Royal Society of Chemistry: Science Research News, extracts for your class: https://edu.rsc.org/science-research-news-extracts-for-your-class/109548.more?navcode=101254

Institute of Physics: Stories from Physics: https://spark.iop.org/stories-physics

Royal Society of Biology: Biology Changing the World, reading and video extracts about great biologists: https://biologyheritage.rsb.org.uk/bcw

Pitfalls to avoid when teaching disciplinary knowledge

Avoid attempting to teach disciplinary knowledge independently of substantive knowledge. Scientific methods are not generalisable life skills that can be studied in isolation. Teaching scientific skills will always be dependent on the scientific context.

For example, science teachers are required to teach the scientific skill of 'measurement', but this is not a stand-alone topic. Instead, each time measurement is taught, the teacher teaches it in the context of the substantive subject content or the lesson topic, for example:

- how to use a spirometer to measure lung volume in biology
- how to use an ammeter to measure electrical current in physics
- how to use a thermometer to measure the change in temperature in exothermic and endothermic reactions in chemistry.

Part of the teacher's role is to make it explicit to their students that scientific choices have been made as to which measuring device to use, and that in doing so, they have been working scientifically:

- You could model this by describing what equipment you have chosen and why: 'I am using an ammeter because that is the equipment scientists use to measure electrical current.'
- You could engage the class in a discussion by proposing an incorrect piece of equipment: 'I need to measure electrical current. As a scientist,

I need to choose the right equipment carefully. I think I'm going to use a voltmeter. Is this experiment going to work?'

■ You could use a hinge question to stimulate discussion of disciplinary knowledge: 'There are lots of ways to measure the volume of this 5 cm³ of liquid accurately. Which would be the most effective equipment to use: a 10 cm³ measuring cylinder, a graduated syringe, a burette or a 5 cm³ volumetric pipette?' After posing the question and getting students to vote, you could facilitate a discussion.

■ At a more advanced level, you could also pose a follow-up question: 'In the context of this experiment, does it matter which of these options we use? What level of inaccuracy is acceptable for this experiment?'

Teaching strategies that are useful for both substantive and disciplinary knowledge

There is a wide overlap between strategies for teaching substantive and disciplinary knowledge, and the best teachers will teach them together. For example, we have seen that retrieval practice and low-stakes testing are useful for explicitly teaching both types of knowledge.

Knowledge organisers

Knowledge organisers can be a helpful tool to summarise core knowledge for a unit of work. An A3 sheet for a topic, including a glossary, visual representation of key processes and summaries of important information, can be useful in lots of ways, but it is crucial to plan to include both substantive and disciplinary knowledge in the information presented.

Knowledge organisers can:

■ make visible links between prior, current and future learning – include a box titled 'Remember this?' to look backwards and one titled 'This will help you with future study' to make forwards links

■ be used by students for revision – specify the cover-and-check method or partner testing

■ be valuable for teachers who are not subject experts, or who are unfamiliar with a topic, to give them confidence that they are covering the curriculum as expected

■ explicitly remind both teachers and pupils of the importance of both substantive and disciplinary knowledge by including both

- be helpful for students – creating their own knowledge organisers can be an excellent way of engaging them with their learning and assessing gaps in their knowledge.

In summary:

- When planning a science curriculum, integrate both substantive and disciplinary knowledge. It helps to explicitly identify both the substantive and disciplinary knowledge you want to teach.
- Key strategies for teaching substantive knowledge include retrieval tasks and low-stakes testing.
- Key strategies for teaching disciplinary knowledge include retrieval tasks, low-stakes testing, well-thought-out explanations and wider reading.
- If you have time to create a knowledge organiser summarising both substantive and disciplinary knowledge for a unit of work, this can be beneficial for both students and teachers.

Experiential knowledge

Types of knowledge can be broken down into three distinct categories: explicit, implicit and experiential (sometimes called tacit knowledge). Explicit knowledge is the facts that are explicitly taught and remembered by students. It makes up the vast amount of the substantive knowledge we aim to teach our students. For instance, when learning about cells in biology, the explicit knowledge we expect our students to gain includes the names of functions of the organelles, the key differences between plant and animal cells, and the adaptations present in cells that have specific functions, for example. Implicit knowledge is the application of explicit knowledge to a situation or problem. When learning about cells, students might be asked to evaluate how a root hair cell is adapted for function. By applying their explicit knowledge – the structure of a root hair cell – students can attempt to answer this question. Experiential (or tacit) knowledge is knowledge gained through experience, by doing things in the real world. Experiential knowledge is often subjective, informal and difficult to share directly.

An example of experiential knowledge can be seen in the television show *The Great British Bake Off*. In the 'technical challenge', contestants are asked to bake a product without being told in advance what it will be. They are given a basic recipe and a time limit, and are asked to produce a number of baked items. Here, the contestants are given explicit knowledge – the recipe for the items they are making. All the bakers have some implicit knowledge as, to get on the show, they must be bakers of a high standard. But the only way to have experiential knowledge is to have had experience of baking the product before. Often, those with the extra experiential knowledge do a better job in this technical challenge.

If they have been asked to make a set of doughnuts, bakers who have experiential knowledge, having made doughnuts before, will understand how the dough will look, feel and behave, in a way that those who have never made doughnuts before will not. Their experience – their experiential knowledge – makes them far better equipped to handle this task.

Why is experiential knowledge important in science teaching?

Experiential knowledge can be extremely useful for students in fixing ideas, concepts and phenomena into their schema of knowledge. Being able to see and influence scientific phenomena creates concrete experiences to which other knowledge and explanation can be linked.

I once taught a Year 7 bottom set science class the topic of cells. I introduced the idea that people, animals and plants are all made up of small individual parts that we can't see. I used an analogy of building things out of LEGO® bricks; the bricks are like the cells and the overall construction is the plant or animal. Finally, we looked at some idealised diagrams of cells and the parts of a cell.

I had made what I thought was a strong case for cells, linking to an idea my students would understand (LEGO®) and covering the knowledge they needed. However, my explanation was met with 'I don't believe this' and 'I can't see these cells' from some of the students.

I had to let these students experience seeing cells for themselves. We got out the microscopes and prepared some onion cell slides. Students went through the process of taking a piece of onion skin, using a microscope and viewing cells for themselves. This experience, when combined with the explicit knowledge I had given the class, allowed students to create a key anchor in their schema of a cell, what one looks like and how they might observe one.

We must be careful with experiential knowledge. Some of the experiential knowledge students bring to lessons conflicts with what we are trying to teach them. Students' experience of the world around them often doesn't quite match up with what they learn in class. For instance, in biology we teach students that plants can make their own food using photosynthesis, but a student may ask 'So why can I buy plant food in a garden centre?'. This misconception is based on the student's tacit knowledge and needs challenging, but it also presents an opportunity to go further than photosynthesis and talk about the other nutrients that plants need (connecting that information to the student's existing knowledge).

How can we promote the acquisition of relevant experiential knowledge?

We need to ensure that we create opportunities for students to experience the ideas and phenomena that we teach them about. This means getting students to *do* things, often through practical work.

In chemistry, when teaching students that increasing the temperature makes a reaction go faster, let students experience this by doing the same chemical reaction at different temperatures (the disappearing cross experiment being an excellent and easy-to-do example). In physics, when teaching Hooke's law, let students experience this by putting some masses onto a spring and seeing what happens.

Data analysis is another opportunity to give students powerful experiential as well as explicit learning. When drawing a graph, it is important to have a scale that is sensible and allows the points to be evenly distributed across the area of the graph. Letting students try this themselves by drawing some graphs, choosing their own scale, making mistakes and iterating gives them this experiential knowledge of how a scale should be, what a graph should look like and what drawing it correctly is like.

Further reading

Counsell, C. (2018) 'Taking Curriculum Seriously', *Impact: Journal of the Chartered College of Teaching*. Available at: https://my.chartered.college/impact_article/taking-curriculum-seriously/

Goldacre, B. (2008) 'Roger Coghill and the Aids Test', *Bad Science* (blog). Available at: https://www.badscience.net/2008/06/roger-coghill-fails-the-aids-test/

CHAPTER 4
HOW DO I SEQUENCE MY CURRICULUM TO BUILD SCHEMAS?

The National Curriculum, GCSE and A-level specifications set out in great detail what should be taught in science lessons. Having such a precise list of content – both substantive and disciplinary – can be very helpful. In other ways, however, this throws up challenges. What order should this content be covered in? What shall we do first? What should be left till later?

There are barriers to learning if content isn't covered in an intentional and thoughtful way: some learning depends on having already mastered other content. You can't simply start teaching specialised cells, for example, without students already having learned about the basics of cell structure. In chemistry, it would be difficult to teach ionic bonding without students having an understanding of atomic structure, particularly the electronic structure of atoms and ions.

In any given lesson, you want learning to be as straightforward as possible. Having a properly sequenced curriculum makes learning easier, by ensuring each lesson is well placed to build on the learning from previous lessons. A well-sequenced curriculum also supports staff, including non-experts and new teachers, to develop their own skills as science teachers, by putting in place a secure structure to support their classroom practice in individual lessons. This does not happen by accident, but through an ongoing process of asking rigorous questions of your curriculum, questions we will look at below before exploring some exemplar curriculums in practice.

Is it a 'science' or a 'biology/physics/chemistry' curriculum?

The science curriculum is in some ways more complicated to plan than that of other subjects, as it is split into three distinct but related subject areas: biology, chemistry and physics. Schools need to consider how to approach this three-in-one subject: should it be taught as 'science', weaving the three areas of biology, chemistry and physics together, or should these be kept separate and distinct? While the substantive knowledge is often specific to an individual subject area, and so may benefit from being kept separate in the curriculum, much of the disciplinary knowledge of science is generally applicable to all three subjects.

The answer to this question of 'separate or together' within the science curriculum relies overwhelmingly on the context of the school, the students you are teaching, the resources available (including the specialities of the teachers available) and the qualifications being studied by the students. The reality for most schools is some kind of hybrid approach, whereby 'science' appears on student timetables, but the topics are clearly broken up into biology, chemistry and physics. This may involve different teachers delivering their specialism (depending on availability), but often also sees some teachers teaching content and topics outside of their subject specialism.

For this complex, three-headed monster of a subject, a well-structured, clearly planned and suitable curriculum is key to supporting teachers (especially those teaching outside of their subject specialism), as well as student learning.

What different types of curriculum work in science?

Two common approaches to structuring programmes of science study are hierarchical curriculums and spiral curriculums.

Hierarchical curriculum

Traditional science curriculums are often hierarchical. A hierarchical curriculum involves students learning a large block of knowledge, usually presented as a topic or unit of work. Later, another block of work will build on this knowledge.

An example of a hierarchical curriculum from chemistry is shown in the table:

Year 7 topic	Year 8 topic	Year 9 topic
The particle model: studying differences between solids, liquids and gases	Elements, mixtures and compounds	Bonding: ionic compounds, covalent compounds and metals

If you are planning a hierarchical curriculum, start by identifying the topics you will cover across a key stage. Then think about the order in which you will teach them. Interrogate your decisions with the following questions:

- How does this topic build on previous ones?
- How does putting this topic here support future learning?
- Why have we decided to start the year with this topic?
- Where are the assessment points in the year?
- Have the topics to be assessed been given sufficient time before the assessment?

Spiral curriculum

A spiral curriculum is one in which core concepts are revisited regularly and developed further. It would be difficult to create a spiral curriculum covering all the National Curriculum substantive knowledge in science. There simply would not be time to *regularly* revisit all the content on the specification. However, a spiral curriculum *can* work well for addressing the big ideas of science and in building disciplinary knowledge.

Take these three bullet points from the National Curriculum content on working scientifically:

- Pupils should be taught to evaluate risks.
- Pupils should be taught to make predictions using scientific knowledge and understanding.
- Pupils should be taught to understand and use SI (Système International) units and IUPAC (International Union of Pure and Applied Chemistry) chemical nomenclature.

Using a spiral curriculum would ensure that students regularly return to these skills in different contexts and subjects, building their expertise over time. We could expect science students to cover these skills in every year – perhaps even every topic – of their study.

Revisiting content should still be mapped intentionally. Repetition in a spiral curriculum does not mean simply duplicating the same thing over and over. It should involve *progression*. When preparing a spiral curriculum, time should be spent mapping the relevant disciplinary skills and thinking about what exactly should be taught at each given point in the curriculum.

For example, the first of the National Curriculum points regarding risk evaluation could be mapped as shown in the table:

Year 7	Year 9	Year 11
Asking students to identify basic risks in practical work, such as burns from a Bunsen burner or knowing acid is corrosive	Developing understanding of safety precautions and proposing their own safety measures	Creating a risk assessment plan – identifying risks, rating them from minimal to severe and suggesting ways to minimise risks

What are threshold concepts and how do they appear in curriculum planning?

Threshold concepts are the necessary prior knowledge a student needs to access new learning. These concepts are important in science as without a base understanding of a concept or model, the more complex knowledge and understanding will be impossible to gain.

For instance, when teaching students about the reactivity of Group 1 metals in chemistry and why their reactivity increases going down the group, threshold concepts will include:

1 constructing the electronic configuration of an atom

2 describing how atoms form ions

3 knowing that subatomic particles have charge.

Without this knowledge, students will be able to observe different levels of reactivity, but not explain them. The knowledge outlined above is a threshold to new knowledge, and without it, students will never be able to make further progress.

To draw the diagrams below, students need to be able to construct the electronic structure of the Group 1 metals (e.g. lithium and sodium) using their prior knowledge:

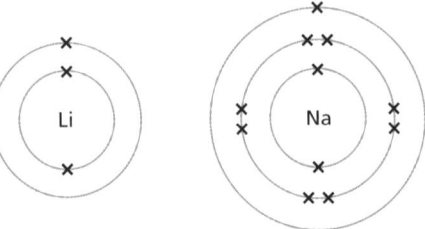

▲ **Figure 2 The electronic structure of lithium and sodium**

Next, access further prior knowledge of the students by asking, 'what are these atoms going to do when they react?'. Ensure students are confident with the knowledge that these atoms will lose an electron to form ions. If students are not clear on these points, stop teaching new content and revisit the content until they are. These are threshold concepts and without them, students will struggle to understand the new learning.

When these two things are learned, the question of why sodium is more reactive (why it more easily loses its electron to form an ion) can be tackled. The answer is that the outer electron in sodium is further from the nucleus so there is less attraction between the oppositely charged particles. Finally, the idea of shielding, the most complicated reason for changes in reactivity, can be tackled.

Without the prior knowledge of atomic structure, electronic structure and formation of ions, this topic would be almost impossible for students to understand. With that prior knowledge, the concept builds to a full explanation of an observed phenomenon.

It is evident from this example that threshold concepts should be clearly identified and carefully considered when planning any science curriculum.

How do you sequence disciplinary learning in the curriculum?

The important thing about sequencing disciplinary learning is to do it *explicitly*; don't just assume that the development of scientific skills will happen through osmosis or by chance. The 2023 Ofsted Curriculum Review for Science in schools found that:

> Leaders' plans to develop pupils' disciplinary knowledge were usually much less developed than their plans to develop pupils' substantive knowledge. In general, not enough consideration was given to identifying the disciplinary knowledge, including concepts, that are needed to work scientifically. This limited how effectively leaders could plan a curriculum for pupils to get better at working scientifically over time. Too often, the focus was simply on identifying practical activities for pupils to complete.

'Doing practicals' is not the same as teaching disciplinary knowledge, although some disciplinary skills can be taught *through* practical work. But just listing when practicals should take place is not a curriculum map of disciplinary skills. Instead, a good curriculum map should identify the disciplinary skills to be learned in each topic and signpost opportunities for these. For each practical in the map, detail the specific disciplinary skills that are the focus of learning (such as accuracy of measuring or using apparatus). In theory lessons, signpost the opportunities to develop disciplinary skills (such as making predictions or analysing data).

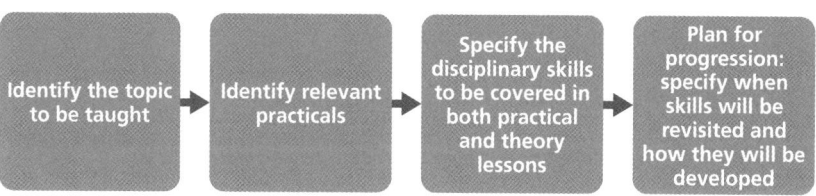

▲ Figure 3 Sequencing disciplinary knowledge

How should assessment be embedded in the science curriculum?

There are two categories of assessment to plan at the curriculum level: firstly, end-of-unit assessments that test what has been learned close to the point of learning; secondly, larger summative assessments which take in multiple topics and are assessed distant from the point of learning. End-of-year exams are often based on a whole-school exam timetable, rather than being at the discretion of different departments.

There are multiple layers of assessment in a curriculum. They can be explained to teachers and pupils using a table as shown here:

	Every lesson	At the end of a unit	At the end of the year
How will the teacher assess me?	Questioning, low-stakes tests	Exam-style questions in exam conditions in the classroom, focused on the unit you have just finished	A formal exam paper sat in the hall in exam conditions, testing all the topics you have done this year
How will this help me improve in science?	Immediate feedback on what I know, so I can make quick improvements to learning in real time	You will be able to practise revising a whole unit and will get better at working in exam conditions Your marked paper will show you what you did well, and what you need to revise further	Revising for a multi-topic exam will help prepare you for GCSE Your marked paper will tell you what topics you have done well, and what needs further revision A report to your parents/carers will give you a grade, so you can see where you are currently performing and targets to improve

It is important for teachers to know the expectations for end-of-unit assessments:

- Is there a window of time in which exams must take place? When must marking be complete? What is the procedure for returning exams to students? Make sure you know the answers to these questions before you start each unit, so you can plan around them.
- Leave enough time for revision; model to students how to revise.
- Make sure you finish the content in time for students to sit the exam.
- Timetable a lesson for feedback with marked papers.

- Even for end-of-unit tests, some moderation is a good idea, possibly by asking teachers to swap three papers with a peer to check the accuracy of their marking.

For end-of-year exams, you will probably have to work around a whole-school timetable. This will have an impact on your curriculum plans. If the end-of-year exam is in June, you will need to structure time for students to revise (and be taught to revise). That might take most of May (with the Easter or half-term holidays) out of contention for teaching new content. And it will leave you with time before the summer holiday without the pressure of looming examinations.

Some key questions to ask when curriculum planning for an end-of-year exam:

- What content absolutely must be covered before the exam?
- What content do you want to revisit before the exam? (consider topics students have not tackled for more than a term)
- What content could productively be left and taught later?

How do you integrate core knowledge and hinterland in the curriculum?

Core knowledge is the subject content you want your students to remember long term. It is the facts you will test, revise and include in recap-and-retrieval tasks. In contrast, hinterland is the term given to the stories that surround these core facts. This is not knowledge that needs to be tested and drilled into long-term memory, but it is the detail and the illustration that brings the subject to life by conveying the real-world context of the learning.

The most widely cited example of the difference between these two types of knowledge is found in chemistry: knowledge of the Haber process is core knowledge, but knowing the story of Fritz Haber himself is hinterland (see Chapter 8 for more on Haber and hinterland teaching).

There are three simple ways to add hinterland to the curriculum:

1 Tell the stories yourself, using your own knowledge of the scientific 'backstory' to engage and inspire the class during the lesson.

2 Set research tasks, possibly as homework, for students to discover interesting stories themselves.

49

3   Source and set reading tasks for students to do. The Dr Wilkinson
    Science blog has stories from science with questions already attached
    and ready to go: https://drwilkinsonscience.wordpress.com/2018/07/05/
    sciencestories/

To bring rigour to your integration, spend some time mapping the
hinterland opportunities across your curriculum. It should not be left
to individual teachers to do this on an *ad hoc* basis, as this will mean
students do not have equality of opportunity between classes.

An example of core and hinterland planning is shown in the table:

Core focus	Hinterland opportunity
Physics: use of ray model to explain imaging in mirrors, the pinhole camera, the refraction of light and action of convex lens in focusing (qualitative)	Reading or research task: the role of Muslim scholars in writing the laws of refraction, especially the work of Ibn al-Haytham
Chemistry: the Haber process	Teacher to tell the story of Fritz Haber
Biology: the development of the DNA model	Research task: find out about the roles played by Watson, Crick, Wilkins and Franklin in the development of the DNA model

This could also be a great opportunity for collaborative planning,
involving all teachers in the department in sharing ideas. Everyone, from
your newest trainee to your most experienced head of department, will
have read and studied different things; put this diversity of experience
to use by asking everyone to contribute some stories to a bank of
hinterland ideas.

What does 'ambition for all' look like in a science curriculum?

Academic aspiration should be baked into teaching science. But what this
looks like will be different for every student. For some students, studying
triple science GCSE and A-levels in multiple sciences is the right path; for
other students, completing a double science GCSE is an achievement to
be celebrated.

Ambition for all in science should focus on engaging every student with the core purposes of science teaching. Every student should:

- be exposed to the wonder and awe of science
- be able to work scientifically and to engage in practical work
- have the chance to learn scientific knowledge (and celebrate that learning)
- be empowered to understand global issues in science and develop their own perspective
- develop an understanding of the diversity of careers in STEM.

To be ambitious for *all* our students is to want them to achieve well, but also for them to have inspiring experiences in their science lessons. Success might be seen in results but should also be seen in the development of students who love science and who look forward to their lessons.

Think about the most challenging groups with the highest barriers to learning: what opportunities have those students got to develop their love of science? What additional opportunities can you provide? With some groups, it can be tempting to hold back on class practicals or demonstrations out of fear of behaviour management challenges. But for students in the most challenging classes, this approach can create even more disengagement, as science is reduced to a textbook-based 'boring' subject. Instead, work with mentors, technicians and department leaders on safety strategies and behaviour approaches so that all students can engage in practicals. The enjoyment, potential for wonder and chance to build relationships through trust and praise will all have positive impacts on student engagement with the subject.

Consider trips, not to push the more able learners, but as a way to build the cultural capital, the engagement and the understanding of working scientifically for all students, ensuring that every student is able to participate. Plan debates on science issues of the day and involve all students. Listen to their perspectives and show them how a scientist approaches these issues. Respect their experience and then add scientific context as part of your ambition to build informed and engaged citizens.

Celebrate success in science learning publicly. Consider an Excellence Exhibition for parents and local communities to see the work students have done. Ensure you consider what excellence means for each child; create opportunities for everyone to shine, from the future doctor to the student who might struggle to get a grade 2 at GCSE but has fought for every mark.

Example in practice: King Edward VI Aston School

King Edward VI Aston School is a selective boys school in the Aston area of Birmingham, UK. All students at the school sit separate science subjects at GCSE and the school has a well-staffed science department (three biologists, five chemists and four physicists).

The school educates approximately 1000 students: 700 in Years 7–11 and about 300 in the sixth form. The school timetables 'science' in Year 7 so that students receive seven 50-minute lessons over a fortnight. After Year 7, teaching is split into biology, chemistry and physics lessons. Students receive three 50-minute lessons a fortnight in Years 8 and 9, five lessons a fortnight in Years 10 and 11, and A-level students in all science subjects receive twelve 50-minute lessons a fortnight. Science is a popular subject for students to choose at A-level. (In Year 12 there are four biology classes, four chemistry classes and three physics classes.)

Classes from Years 8–11 have one teacher, a specialist in the subject area being taught, who delivers all the content. In Years 12 and 13, the lessons and content are normally split across two teachers.

Each department writes its own subject-intent documents, and plans the order, content and style of delivery. While the three subject areas operate independently, there is a strong tradition and commitment to working collaboratively between the departments. The Year 7 curriculum is decided jointly across the three subject areas and is intended to serve as an introduction to secondary science for students within the school. During Year 7, the focus is on building disciplinary knowledge, practical skills and maths skills and introducing students to the key big ideas that underlie the three subject areas. Lessons in Year 7 are often split across two teachers, with teachers covering their specialism where possible.

Content overview: KS3 chemistry

Year 7	Year 8	Year 9
Taught as part of the wider Year 7 science curriculum	**Taught by one teacher**	**Taught by one teacher**
Working scientifically	**Elements, mixtures and compounds**	**The Earth and its atmosphere**
Understanding experimental and investigative skills, including measuring, analysing and evaluating Maths, data analysis and graph skills in science	Definitions of elements, mixtures and compounds Separating techniques Chromatography	The evolution of the Earth's atmosphere The composition and structure of the current atmosphere Structure of the Earth The rock cycle Human impact on the atmosphere
States of matter	**Properties of metals and alloys**	**Atomic structure**
The particle model of solids, liquids and gases Changing of states Diffusion and pressure	Classifying substances as metals or non-metals What is an alloy? Why do we produce alloys?	A simple (Dalton) atomic model Development of the atomic model through time Evidence for this atomic model Subatomic particles Electronic structure of atoms and ions →

Year 7 Taught as part of the wider Year 7 science curriculum	Year 8 Taught by one teacher	Year 9 Taught by one teacher
The Periodic Table, an introduction	**Reactions of metals**	**The Periodic Table**
How the Periodic Table is arranged Metals and non-metals in the Periodic Table What is an element; how is it different to a mixture or a compound?	The reactions of metals with acids Naming salts formed from the reactions of metals and acids Writing word equations The reactivity series Displacement reactions	The development of the Periodic Table The principles underpinning the Mendeleev periodic periods and groups; metals and non-metals; how patterns in reactions can be predicted
Chemical reactions	**Chemical formulae and balanced equations**	**Groups in the Periodic Table**
The difference between chemical and physical changes Dissolving and solubility Combustion and the fire triangle Testing for different gases	Use of chemical symbols Formulae of chemical compounds (specifically ionic compounds) Writing balanced symbol equations for reactions	Group 1 – reactions, properties and uses Group 7 – reactions, properties and uses Transition metals – reactions, properties and uses The noble gases – reactions, properties and uses →

Year 7 **Taught as part of the wider Year 7 science curriculum**	Year 8 **Taught by one teacher**	Year 9 **Taught by one teacher**
Acids and alkalis	**The Earth's resources**	**Chemical bonding**
Classifying compounds as acids and alkalis Using indicators Natural indicators Neutralisation reactions	Finite and infinite resources Reduction of waste through recycling Life cycle assessments of products	Why elements form bonds The different types of bonds formed How the structure and type of bonding affects the properties of materials Know specific examples of bonding
Environmental chemistry	**Materials**	**Chemical changes**
How recycling and reusing products is important How to plan for the life of a product How we are starting to change the world through our waste The effects of some of our waste on the world	Ceramics Composites Polymers Properties and uses of these things	Formation of salts and the reactions of metals and acids, etc. Understand how the reactivity series can be used to predict reactions How metals react to form positive ions
	Jobs in chemistry	
	What kind of jobs are available in chemistry? What skills are needed for these jobs? How do these jobs affect the world around us?	

As the subject areas at this school operate essentially as three linked but separate departments, we will focus on the chemistry curriculum at KS3.

How does the school approach progression in curriculum planning?

The curriculum is designed so that topics in Year 8 rely on and build on knowledge from Year 7 and topics in Year 9 rely on and build on knowledge from Year 8. This hierarchical nature allows for new knowledge to be built on solid foundational knowledge from previous years, but also for students to revisit and reinforce previous knowledge. In this way, the curriculum becomes a progression.

For instance, we can see a clear thread running from Year 7 to Year 9 about atoms, elements and compounds. This starts in Year 7 with the core underlying concept of the particle model. This is then expanded on in Year 8, with the idea that particles can be elements or compounds, and that these can be mixtures. Then in Year 9, the idea of bonding is introduced. Each topic builds on the last and offers the perfect opportunity to recap and consolidate the learning from previous topics and years.

The big ideas of each subject are threaded through the curriculum, to be revisited every year. For instance, in chemistry, the idea of chemical reactions is a running thread. In Year 7, students learn to define a chemical reaction and look at neutralisation reactions. This is then built on in Year 8, by looking at reactions of metals and building balanced symbol equations. Finally, these ideas and skills can be fully applied in Year 9, through reactions in Groups 1 and 7 and the topic of chemical changes.

How does the curriculum look, both forwards and backwards?

When the curriculum structure was planned, themes and threads of knowledge across topics were identified and used to help sequence the learning. Many topics naturally build on one another. Placing them in order across a key stage allows knowledge to be built up logically and also allows topics to be revisited from one year to the next, checking on and expanding on the students' learning each year.

This can be seen in the teaching of KS3 chemistry. In Year 7, students learn about the particle model and solids, liquids and gases; in Year 8, this is revisited and expanded to cover elements, compounds, molecules and mixtures. These ideas form the foundational knowledge for many Year 9 topics but are particularly applicable to atomic structure and bonding.

For each topic, we clearly identify – for staff and students – links to prior topics, outlining the knowledge we expect students to have. In lessons that introduce a new topic, we start by priming the students using low-stakes assessment of expected prior knowledge; we then revisit this knowledge before building on it in the new topic.

How does the curriculum promote careers in science?

The curriculum across the three science areas seeks to promote different careers and opportunities in science at all levels. It is both integrated in the normal teaching of topics in all three sciences and looked at explicitly as a topic in its own right.

The goal of all the careers-focused work done in the classroom is to widen the students' knowledge of the opportunities available through the study of science in school and beyond. This is particularly important as developing student understanding of the variety of career opportunities is a key goal for teachers at King Edward VI Aston School.

When planning the curriculum, careers that are specific and applicable to certain topics were highlighted; for instance, the role of a forensic scientist was introduced when teaching analytical chemistry and an engineering career was mentioned when looking at forces. The role, qualifications needed and contributions of these careers are discussed in the class in the context of the topic being taught. Integrating discussion of careers and job roles into substantive teaching helps to make the learning real for students, allowing them to see the real-world impact of their learning.

In addition, all students spend time in Year 8 researching careers and presenting their findings back to their classes. In each of the three sciences, students are given a career to research: they find out about the qualifications needed to do this role, what the day-to-day job looks like, the areas of science that the role employs and other interesting details.

How does the curriculum plan approach practicals?

When the curriculum was planned, the key practical opportunities for each topic were identified and put into the curriculum plan. These identified practicals are highly recommended to individual classroom teachers, but do not represent the only investigations that students are expected to complete.

A lot of autonomy is given to teachers to choose what, when and in what format they do practical work with their students. We believe that teachers know their students best and so can adapt practical work to suit their classes. There is a clear understanding that practicals must fit with what students are doing and that practical work to fill time or simply for the sake of it is not encouraged.

Teachers think about and share the best ways to carry out practical work, asking the questions: 'Is this best done by students or as a demonstration?' and 'What do I want my students to learn from this practical?'.

Example in practice: Dame Elizabeth Cadbury School

Dame Elizabeth Cadbury is a non-selective secondary school in Birmingham, UK, which had 825 students on the roll in 2023. It is part of the Matrix Academy Trust and has a sixth form. In 2023, 38.2% of students were eligible for free school meals, compared to a national average of 23.8%. Despite this indicator of economic disadvantage, the school achieved a Progress 8 score of 0.19, compared to 0.07 for state-funded schools in the Birmingham Local Authority, and the national average score of –0.03. In Year 11, 14% of students take single sciences rather than double award science.

The school sets out its golden rule: if it would not be good enough for our own staff's relatives, it is not good enough for Dame Elizabeth pupils.

The science faculty is comprised of 10 members of staff, supported by two technicians. There is a range of experience within the faculty, as well as staff who have previously worked in industry. The three science disciplines are represented equally among the staff and all are offered as A-levels within the growing sixth form. We are fortunate to have four hours' teaching time per week in KS3, allowing us to develop substantive and disciplinary knowledge in depth and using feedback regularly to support students. This also enables us to teach transition units at the end of Year 9, with a clear focus on linking the core concepts together to secure prior knowledge and then build on it in a more synoptic manner. As part of this, we are currently developing further transition units that will allow this process to be even smoother, based on student needs in KS4. Our current focus is to develop a transition unit on bonding that introduces the topic in a KS3 context, rather than its introduction occurring at GCSE level.

Content overview: KS3 science

Year	Teacher 1	Teacher 2
7	**The particle model**	**Forces**
	This is a topic that builds on the KS2 curriculum and so acts as an excellent introduction to Year 7 science. We check prior knowledge, address misconceptions and build from there. There are also lots of opportunities to introduce disciplinary knowledge.	This is a topic that is included in the KS2 curriculum and is very tangible, with lots of checks for misconceptions and introduction of disciplinary knowledge within the KS3 National Curriculum.
	Mixtures and separation	**Energy**
	This topic enables revisiting of KS2 content and building on this to include some interleaving of the Particles topic. Lots of practical opportunities.	This is not covered explicitly in the KS2 curriculum and so provides an opportunity to build a key strand of physics from scratch. There is an important element of checking and addressing 'real-world' misconceptions during this unit.
	Cells, tissues and organs	**Current electricity**
	This is a tough topic that includes lots of terminology, diagrams and skills (including preparing a microscope slide). The skills are carefully integrated with consideration given to cognitive load.	This topic is included in the KS2 curriculum, however, the focus of this unit is to formalise the concepts and terminology introduced previously. This is also a good opportunity to get students used to the circuit apparatus that they will use throughout KS3 and KS4.
	Sexual reproduction in animals	**Atoms, elements and molecules**
	This is placed here as it supports the whole-school RSE (relationships and sex education) programme and builds on the KS2 science and RSE curriculums.	This introduces key concepts that are used throughout KS3 and KS4 but also gives an opportunity for interleaving of the Mixtures topic. →

Year	Teacher 1	Teacher 2
	Muscles and bones	**Acids and alkalis**
	This topic builds on the Cells topic and looks at organ systems, including the skeleton and muscles, before branching out into the respiratory and circulatory systems. Specialised cells are also recapped in this unit, with specific examples integrated into larger organ systems (e.g. muscle cells).	This topic allows many of the previous topics to be seen in a specific context that can then be broadened to everyday and industrial use. The opportunity to develop disciplinary knowledge through study of indicators is used extensively throughout this topic.
	Ecosystems	**Sound**
	This topic is closely linked to KS2 but is taught here as it allows opportunities for sampling outdoors rather than in a classroom.	This topic introduces quite a wide range of concepts compared to other Year 7 units. It builds on KS2 but includes use of units (Hz etc.), as well as linking to the concept of energy transfers and formalising waves ahead of the Light topic in Year 8.
8	**Food and nutrition**	**Energy transfers**
	This topic builds on some of the Body systems topics taught in Year 7 (as well as in the KS2 curriculum). It is also placed here as it builds on the Year 7 Food technology curriculum and links into the Year 8 content in this area (balanced diets etc.).	This topic is predominantly about heat as an energy transfer. There are opportunities to address misconceptions and build formal knowledge of conduction, convection and radiation (which are considered assumed prior knowledge within our GCSE specification). The Year 7 Energy topic is interleaved alongside knowledge from the KS2 curriculum. →

Year	Teacher 1	Teacher 2
	The Periodic Table	**Combustion**
	This unit builds on the Elements and atoms topic, as well as introducing the Periodic Table. There are lots of opportunities for cultural capital within this unit, including Mendeleev and Marie Curie.	As well as the clear link to atoms, elements and compounds in Year 7, this unit is closely linked to the Energy and Energy transfers topics. This is also where basic symbol equations are used to build on the word equations encountered previously. Comparing fuels is also in this topic and is used to develop conclusions based on numerical data as disciplinary knowledge (alongside the use of apparatus).
	Plants and their reproduction	**Light**
	Plant structure is included in the KS2 curriculum to a basic level. There is interleaving with the Sexual reproduction topic in Year 7, as well as with the Ecosystems topic.	This topic builds on sound with the concept of waves as an energy transfer. Topics from KS2 are formalised. This topic has also been placed here to allow mutual support with maths regarding use of protractors and measuring angles against a reference line.
	Rocks	**Metals and their uses**
	This topic builds on the geography topic that happens at the same time with examples shared and specific elements (e.g. intrusive and extrusive rocks) given greater focus and depth in particular subjects. For example, the rock cycle is taught but students are reminded of the link to plate boundaries and the processes that they are taught in geography.	This topic allows a lot of interleaving with previous chemistry topics, including the Periodic Table and Acids. Word and symbol equations are used here, having been introduced in previous topics. Design and use of metal products is also taught in Design and Technology (DT) at this point, so there are links made between scientific knowledge (e.g. metals and alloys) and DT theory and design. →

Year	Teacher 1	Teacher 2
	Breathing and respiration	**Fluids**
	This unit is based around linking the organ systems that have been introduced previously to the chemical reactions topics taught earlier. In this respect, it is our first true 'biochemistry' unit, and these links are taught explicitly with prior knowledge checked and reinforced.	This unit links the particle model and forces. Throughout the topic, these two core science concepts are used to explain phenomena (such as floating) that have been taught or seen before.
	Unicellular organisms	**Earth and space**
	This unit builds on the Cells unit as well as ecology (especially the role of unicellular organisms as decomposers). This unit explicitly teaches life beyond the plants and animals that have been the focus thus far. It also introduces (without detail regarding mitosis) the concept of asexual reproduction, building on the two Sexual reproduction topics covered earlier in KS3.	This topic is at the point in the year where we often have extra enrichment time so we can expand beyond the National Curriculum (e.g. use of the Liverpool telescope). The main focus of the unit is to link concepts such as seasons and orbits to previous concepts in KS3 such as forces and light. This unit also includes opportunities to explore how scientific models change based on evidence (e.g. the heliocentric and geocentric models) as cultural capital and disciplinary knowledge. →

Year	Teacher 1	Teacher 2
9	**Genetics and evolution**	**Forces and motion**
	This topic reintroduces variation (which is in the KS2 National Curriculum), addressing any misconceptions and clarifying keywords. This is then linked to competition (and ecosystems in Year 7). This allows opportunities for developing graphs of different types of variation (graph skills have been well developed in maths by this point). This is then linked to evolution. DNA, chromosomes and genes are introduced but not in detail as this makes linking the concepts together far more challenging.	This topic builds on the Forces topics previously introduced and links them together by introducing work (an energy transfer), as well as balanced and unbalanced forces and graphs of motion. The focus of this unit is scientific diagrams of the concepts previously taught (building on graph work completed in maths, including the concept of gradients).
	Materials	**Reactivity**
	This unit is strongly linked to the DT curriculum, especially concepts that have been developed in KS3 and are then developed further in KS4. To this end, the National Curriculum points are strongly linked to usage of materials in real-world applications, rather than simple definitions and properties.	Much like the Combustion topic in Year 8, this topic focuses on using data to determine reactivity. This unit also reinforces word and symbol equations, as well as using the particle model to help explain observations. As in the Materials topic, usage of metals in real-world applications is also linked to their reactivity. →

Year	Teacher 1	Teacher 2
	Plant growth	**Forcefields and electromagnets**
	This topic follows up on the Cells and Plant reproduction topics to look at systems within a plant, especially how specialised cells such as root hair cells enable effective water transport within a plant. It is also where photosynthesis is introduced in the context of the entire plant, including how reactants are acquired.	Since the reintroduction of more detailed work on magnetism and magnetic fields in GCSE, we have expanded this topic to include a proper introduction to field diagrams (including arrows) as well as plotting compasses.
	Key concepts in biology	**States of matter and separation techniques**
	This topic links directly to the previous Cells topic and provides opportunities to deepen learning and check for any remaining misconceptions.	This topic revisits concepts that have not been explicitly taught since Year 7. Misconceptions are checked and the particle model is recapped, with greater focus on the motion of particles.
	Energy transfers and stores	**Atomic structure and the Periodic Table**
	In this unit, qualitative calculations are added to the previous qualitative introduction to energy, especially the working out method we use that is consistent within the faculty. There is a strong link here to KS3 science and geography in terms of energy resources and the change in use.	In this unit, students build on their previous knowledge from Years 7 and 8 with a more detailed annotation of the Periodic Table (such as names of groups), along with atomic structure. The language introduced in this unit is the same as that used in the radioactivity topic in Year 10.
		Motion
		This topic builds on the one taught earlier in Year 9, including the graphs of motion. In this unit, speed–time graphs (including gradients and areas) are added.

Key questions

At Dame Elizabeth Cadbury, curriculum planning is structured around six key questions, which are considered below.

1 How can we plan for disciplinary knowledge to be explicitly developed through the curriculum?
The first step is to clearly map disciplinary knowledge through the curriculum, so that all teachers know *what* needs to be taught *when*. The curriculum plan sets out consistent strategies and techniques for disciplinary skills, so that all teachers approach things the same way. It is important that scaffolding is removed over time and so the level of scaffolding is also mapped. Disciplinary knowledge is assessed, students are given feedback and learning is tracked. The staff have learned from the core practical assessment at A-level, especially how specific skills are chosen for explicit teaching and focused assessment.

2 How can links between subjects support science teaching?
Time is spent sharing curriculum maps and strategies between departments. Geography, DT and physical education (PE) have been particularly productive for creating links. An important discussion with other departments is to ask, 'who does what best?' and then plan for this to be delivered first. If the DT department does a brilliant job teaching gears and levers, plan for this to happen before it happens in science – making the science teacher's job easier! There are some elements which must be done in a science-specific way, from correct use of vocabulary to appropriate methods for graphs. We are clear what these elements are.

3 How do we approach split groups to maximise the quality and efficiency of science teaching?
Our staffing model means that all groups are split. We try to timetable staff so they have multiple classes of one year group with the same split, so that they can teach the same content multiple times. This has a number of benefits:

- it is easy to target CPD when staff need extra support
- staff develop skills in differentiation
- it minimises workload through duplicated planning
- more staff teach in their subject specialism
- efficient development of resources, as one staff member is responsible for teaching a scheme to multiple classes, and in so doing improves the associated resources for others to use.

4 How do we sequence learning to build on prior knowledge?
We approach the science curriculum in a hierarchical manner but paying particular attention to increasing challenge. We start with physics units in Year 7, as our students tend to have done a lot of physics at primary school, so this builds on their prior knowledge and gives a positive first experience of science.

5 How do we integrate careers awareness into the science curriculum?
We have included associated careers within every scheme of work, as well as planning in some additional lessons focusing on the breadth of STEM careers. We have focused time in lessons to look at these. We prioritise local examples and labour force information, including the qualifications students need for a particular career. We choose careers that act as aspiration for the context of our students.

6 How can we use reading to develop cultural capital?
We see reading as a key tool for developing cultural capital around science as a field. All reading tasks are supported by glossaries and, if texts are pitched at too high a reading level, we use ChatGPT to rewrite them with a lower reading age. We use these reading tasks for learning about scientists, BAME (Black, Asian and Minority Ethnic) issues in science and WISE (Women in Science and Engineering). Reading texts are shared with all teachers through shared planning.

Further reading

Boxer, A. 'Core and hinterland: What's what and why it matters'. A Chemical Orthodoxy: Schools, Science and Education (blog). Available at: https://achemicalorthodoxy.co.uk/2019/02/01/core-and-hinterland-whats-what-and-why-it-matters/

Myatt, M. and Tomsett, J. (2001) Huh: Curriculum conversations between subject and senior leaders. Woodbridge: John Catt Educational Ltd.

Myatt, M. 'Science', Mary Myatt (blog). Available at: https://www.marymyatt.com/science

Ofsted (2023) Finding the Optimum: The science subject report. Available at: https://www.gov.uk/government/publications/subject-report-series-science/finding-the-optimum-the-science-subject-report--2#main-findings

Wilkinson, B. 'Dr Wilkinson – Science Teacher Blog' https://drwilkinsonscience.wordpress.com/2018/07/05/sciencestories/

CHAPTER 5
HOW DO I PLAN A SUCCESSFUL SCIENCE LESSON?

Science is a subject full of complex abstract ideas that may seem to bear little direct relation to students' life experiences. It is a dense subject to teach, with lots of subject matter to cover in the curriculum. There are a few important implications of this that science teachers need to recognise when planning lessons.

Firstly, the quality and time given to teacher explanations should be a crucial part of any lesson design in science. New and experienced teachers can both benefit from scripting and refining their explanations before lessons. If you are being observed, ask the observer to focus on the quality of your explanation: can they identify any areas you could make clearer?

Secondly, teachers must acknowledge and plan for the limits imposed by the cognitive load of the material being presented. Repetitive lesson design, in which lessons follow a predictable sequence, can help students by ensuring working memory is focused on the scientific content, rather than on working out how to engage with a new activity.

Thirdly, teachers must recognise the limits of working memory. Repetition of core learning should be part of every lesson, revising substantive and disciplinary knowledge from the last lesson, the last week, the last month and the last year. Only with repetition can students move learning into long-term memory, so the repetition of key learning must be an explicit part of each lesson.

Finally, direct instruction is a powerful tool in science teaching. Enquiry-based learning as a scientific methodology has its place in the science classroom (read more about Mode B teaching on the following page), but in general its weaknesses outweigh its benefits. Direct instruction is a methodology well-suited to a subject where the answers are generally known, where the cognitive load of enquiry-based learning can be daunting and inescapable, and where novice learners are not equipped to draw out valid learning from their own enquiries.

What do Mode A and Mode B teaching look like in a science lesson?

Mode A teaching is best understood as routine, teacher-led lesson design. Outlined by Tom Sherrington in *The Learning Rainforest*, this approach to lesson design is driven by a focus on direct instruction, explicit teacher input and a clear sequence of learning that involves the core skills of 'explain, model, practice, question, assess, feedback and review'. Day-to-day lesson design should be fairly repetitive to reduce the teacher's planning load and the cognitive load for the student. Most of this chapter will focus on Mode A teaching approaches.

Sometimes, however, we want to scatter some stardust, or some chemical adventure, into our classrooms. In Mode B teaching we have space to do things in the classroom that we believe students should get to experience; things that have value for their own sake and that the individual teacher is passionate about. These lessons should still be underpinned by robust teaching practices, but lesson design might be more flexible to accommodate the nature of the tasks. Mode B teaching might be understood as enrichment, except that it should not be thought of as 'bolt on' in the way enrichment is sometimes added in schools.

Sherrington (2017) argues for a very rough 80/20 Mode A : Mode B split of teaching – both are important to the development of students as fully rounded and engaged scientists. This chapter on lesson design will focus on Mode A teaching, through the lens of direct instruction.

What does direct instruction look like in a science lesson?

Rosenshine's model of direct instruction (2012) is a set of principles of effective classroom pedagogy taken from his meta-analysis of findings from three fields of research: the practice of master teachers, cognitive science, and studies into cognitive supports. He formulated his findings into 10 key principles that his research suggested underpin effective classroom instruction:

1 daily review

2 present new material using small steps

3 ask questions

4 provide models

5 guide student practice

6 check for student understanding

7 obtain a high success rate

8 provide scaffolds for difficult tasks

9 independent practice

10 weekly and monthly reviews.

A tremendous amount has been written about Rosenshine's principles in the last few years, and this study has assumed tremendous importance in the educational world for its validity, clarity and ease of use. Here, we will examine the principles of special importance for science teachers.

Recall and retrieval

Part of the challenge of learning science is that there is a lot to remember. In any given class, part of the lesson will be the introduction of new knowledge. Students will use their working memory to engage with the new learning. However, working memory is finite and fickle. As students leave the room, and go home at the end of the day, the learning from the lesson will fade and be lost.

How do we overcome this? By ensuring that every lesson design includes explicit activities asking students to remember learning from yesterday, last week, last month, even last year.

In the 1880s Ebbinghaus proposed his 'Forgetting curve', a model of how learning fades over time, emphasising that memories fade without repetition and that the most rapid knowledge loss happens straight after learning. Daily review is vital: students are most likely to forget what they have just learned, and so almost immediate review is essential.

Try these simple activities to build review of learning into your lessons:

1 a 'Do Now' activity, a brief recap as students enter the room, as described by Doug Lemov in *Teach Like a Champion*

2 a recap grid of nine quick questions, three from yesterday, three from last week and three from last month

3 a Kahoot!, a Blooket game or other online quiz

4 a silent plenary of recap questions.

Modelling

Modelling is a core skill for science teachers; the range of things they need to model effectively is vast. Science teachers need to ensure that they model how to:

- do a practical
- write like a scientist, for example when writing up reports or posters
- read scientific material
- talk like a scientist
- work mathematically in a scientific context
- problem solve in science
- answer complex exam questions
- be safe in a science laboratory or during a practical.

The first thing for science teachers to think about in their lesson design is 'what should I model in this lesson?'. Once the modelling – and there might be multiple moments of modelling in any lesson – is identified, the same principles and processes can be applied to ensure that the modelling is effective.

Should modelling be live or pre-planned?

Both types of modelling have their place in science, but the one you choose will depend on the context. In general, live modelling is useful if you want to explain your thinking processes in real time to students. A pre-planned model can save you time in a lesson, enabling you to address key points with speed.

Live modelling	Pre-planned modelling
• How to do a practical • How to read a scientific article to pick out the key points • Demonstrating a mathematical process with a worked example	• A longer answer to an exam question • How to write a science report

Whichever form of modelling you are deploying, use this checklist to ensure it is helpful and well-structured:

- Be explicit about what you are modelling and say why it is important. What will the students be able to do when they learn this skill?

- Break the skill down into steps.
- Demonstrate how to do each step – whether this by showing it in real time or by asking students to copy you.
- As you model, verbalise your thinking. Say why you are doing it that way, so that pupils develop an understanding of the 'why' as well as the 'what'.
- Point out common mistakes and misconceptions – and how to avoid these.
- And most importantly, as soon as you have finished modelling the task, give the students time to practise it themselves, exactly as you have shown them (mirroring Rosenshine's point 9, independent practice).

What is the role of textbooks in lesson design?

The use of textbooks in science classrooms is an often-debated subject. While textbooks exist that cover the National Curriculum, and all of the GCSE and A-level specifications, their use in the classroom is often condemned by teachers as lazy, uninventive and uninspiring. They are tools used either as a punishment ('listen to me or we will be copying out of a textbook') or saved for cover lessons when the teacher is absent. However, like all resources in the classroom, textbooks are not intrinsically good or bad; used in the correct way, they can be a powerful tool for learning.

The problems with textbooks lie in the tasks we set when using them. All too often, we ask students to read or make notes on a page or a collection of pages from the textbook, and then answer the questions at the end. This search-and-find style of learning means that students will scan through the text focused on finding only the answer to the question asked, while discarding any other information as they go. This is a low level of cognitive demand. For instance, a GCSE chemistry student tasked with reading about the Haber process to answer the question 'what are the conditions for the Haber process?' will learn little from the text beyond '450 degrees Celsius and 200 atmospheres'.

We need to give students a strong purpose with a significant cognitive demand when using a textbook. To do this, we should see a textbook as either a starting point, providing background for a task about to happen, or as supporting material to help answer additional questions that arise during a learning activity. In this way, the use of a textbook in the classroom would mirror the use of an academic text for a professional scientist. For example, when carrying out a hands-on task, such as a practical, students often have questions. Encourage students to write down their questions, then ask them to use the textbook to find the answers. This gives students a meaningful reason for reading the textbook (finding answers to their own questions) and will result in a better overall understanding.

Textbooks can be used effectively to set tasks with cognitive challenge:

- Give students open questions (such as 'how ...'), rather than simple comprehension questions (such as 'what ...').
- Produce a provocative statement and ask students for their view. Instruct them to find evidence in the textbook for and against their conclusion.
- Use the textbook as just one of several reading resources, asking students to draw conclusions across the range of available texts.

Tasks like these encourage students to think deeply about what is being presented to them.

How do I scaffold my lesson design to support students with additional needs effectively?

The mantra 'good teaching for students with special educational needs and disabilities (SEND) is good teaching for all' is empowering for teachers, as it reminds us that supporting students with additional needs is not about adding extra, or onerous, elements to lesson design. Just do the basics well.

The EEF guide *Special Educational Needs in Mainstream Schools* (2020) identifies teaching practices for every lesson, most of which are straightforward for science teachers to implement. In many cases, these will be the core of good practice anyway! Let's examine what these five strategies look like in a science context.

1 Flexible grouping

This strategy is particularly important in organising groups for practical work. Know your students well and organise the groups for practical work to positively support student needs. The possible groupings will be endlessly varied based on the needs of your students and can be tweaked regularly.

2 Cognitive and metacognitive approaches

Help your students organise and recall knowledge with cognitive and metacognitive strategies:

■ Use mnemonics (for example, MRS GREN for characteristics of living things), dual coding, analogies, checklists, graphic organisers and clear methods as cognitive supports.

■ Explicitly teach students how to plan, monitor and evaluate their work, and test them on their knowledge of these strategies to build metacognitive skills.

■ Scaffold learning for students with SEND by making the strategy as explicit as possible. Put the strategies on displays, on coloured paper handouts and in planners.

3 Explicit instruction

Make your teaching as clear and unambiguous as possible. Rosenshine's model of direct instruction is an example of explicit instruction. Using these principles to design lessons will support learners with SEND, as well as providing high-quality teaching for all.

4 Use technology

If setting reading texts, look for opportunities for students to read on a screen. Immersive Reader on Microsoft has a host of intuitive and easy-to-use functions designed to support reading, from highlighting text as it is read to having a voice read the text aloud.

Share a presentation with students in advance of the lesson, so they can read materials in advance, lowering the cognitive load.

5 Scaffolding strategies

Useful scaffolds in science include:

■ checklists of any stepwise processes (such as a printout of steps for a practical)

■ glossaries of vocabulary

■ verbal discussion of a task before starting it, to rehearse ideas.

Don't forget to remove the scaffolds over time, so that students gradually learn to work independently.

How do I relate learning to student experiences as part of my lesson design?

For many students, the ideas and knowledge presented to them during science lessons will seem divorced from their everyday lives and experiences. This sense of distance can make science seem irrelevant and hard to digest. The job of the science teacher is to highlight real-life links explicitly, connecting often abstract and difficult-to-understand ideas to concrete parts of the students' everyday experience.

For example, when learning about equilibrium in GCSE chemistry, students might think, why do I care which way the equilibrium moves? What does it have to do with me? To overcome this, you could set the lesson in terms of a scenario that they would understand. You could ask them to place themselves in the position of a factory owner who wants to get the most out of their factory. How can their factory make the most money? By getting the most stuff to sell. How can they get the most stuff to sell? By producing the most product. How can they get the most product? Well, by using Le Chatelier's principle to maximise the yield.

Here we are using a concept that students can relate to – a business wanting to make money – as a context to support understanding of a difficult, abstract idea in chemistry.

How do I build effective feedback into my lesson design?

Feedback is essential for improving pupil outcomes (the EEF summarises feedback as having an effect size of +6 months), but to be effective, it must be planned with care. Acknowledge that students might be strong in one area and weak in another. Feedback must be a constant feature of lesson design, as you continually seek to discover the extent of pupil understanding *in this specific area of study.*

Mini whiteboards work well in science lessons. Give every child a whiteboard, a pen and an eraser, and pose a question. Students record their answers and – on a count of three – display their boards so the teacher can check every answer simultaneously. Choose boards with incorrect answers and bring them to the front – can the rest of the class work out why they are wrong? Can they spot the misconception?

Hinge questions are great for probing the extent of pupil understanding, but they need careful planning and a PowerPoint to display them. A good hinge question has three plausible answers but only one truly accurate answer. By asking the students to finger vote and then explain why they chose their answer, the teacher can probe the reasons for their choices in detail. Consider this example.

Question: What would you use to look at cells from a plant root?

Possible answers:

1 A telescope

2 A microscope

3 A magnifying glass

4 My eyes

In this case, the right answer is 2. Students might mix up the prefixes and pick 1, which is an opportunity to draw their attention to the prefix 'micro' meaning 'small' and 'tele' meaning 'far off'. This will improve scientific literacy for other words they may meet later. Asking students why a microscope is better than a magnifying glass will enable you to make explicit that microscopes have higher resolution and higher (and adjustable) magnification.

Mini-quizzes

Mini-quiz, pop quiz, recap test: whatever you call them, the more often you build quick, independent tests into your lesson, the more accurately you will understand what pupils know.

In 'low-stakes testing' the emphasis is on removing the stress and intensity of a formal test by making it such a routine part of pupil learning that students will happily engage. How do you make a test 'low stakes'?

■ Explicitly tell pupils you are doing the test to find out gaps in what they know so you can reteach it.

■ Pitch the test so that there are some questions all students will be able to answer – no one enjoys a test where they score 1/10.

■ Deliver the test with humour and positivity.

■ Give no prior warning – a low-stakes test is not one that requires hours of revision.

■ Consider the consequences. If a low-stakes test is for learning, then a detention is not an appropriate response to a low score. After the test, set an activity to address lack of knowledge and close the gap.

How do you provide feedback to the students after a mini-test?

	Self mark	Peer mark	Teacher mark
Advantages	Quick, builds self-evaluation skills	Students will accept criticism from a peer more easily than from a teacher Students can learn from each other's mistakes	Accuracy Excellent teacher understanding of whole-class areas of weakness
Disadvantages	Students need to be trained to get it right The teacher must follow up with a check in to find out which questions caused problems	Students need to be trained to get it right Teacher must follow up with a check in to find out which questions caused problems	Time consuming

Marks or comments?

In *Science Teaching*, Black and Harrison (2004) found that teachers lean towards giving marks as a preferred method of feedback. However, for many students, marks are demotivating and, moreover, they are ill-equipped to follow up by transferring marks into concrete improvement actions. It is, therefore, important to offer qualitative, comment-based feedback to students to help them understand exactly what they need to do to improve.

You could do this through marking a task in an exercise book and offering comments:

■ WWW – what went well
■ EBI – even better if …

However, this can be very time consuming.

Alternatively, you could do this by sharing whole-class feedback, having read through (but not commented individually) on student books. Such feedback might include:

- class strengths
- individual shout outs
- class areas to improve
- key vocabulary to revise.

Individual feedback can also be given verbally in a lesson. For example, when talking about a graph: 'That looks like a really good straight line on your x-axis and you've labelled it perfectly, but don't forget to label the y-axis as well.'

How do I set appropriate homework tasks?

Science is no different from any other subject in that high-quality, relevant and accessible homework is a strong tool for driving students forward in their learning and understanding of the subject.

Homework should be applicable and relevant to the learning taking place in the classroom. All too often, teachers feel the need to set homework because a calendar or plan says that it must be set on a particular day. It is better not to set homework than to set something just for the sake of it.

In science, the best homework exercises are ones in which either the student gets to practise and embed the learning they have done in the class, or the task sets them up for the coming lesson. For example, we might use questions that ask students to recall the information presented during the lesson. These questions could be worksheet based, but increasingly, the availability of online, self-marking quizzes makes this style of homework easier and more powerful for both the student and the teacher. These types of quiz allow for instant feedback to the learner and take the marking load off the teacher, as well as being strong analytical tools for teachers. There are a number of ready-to-go, paid-for services (http://www.educake.co.uk, http://www.samlearning.com, with http://www.drfrostmaths.com and http://www.exampro.co.uk due to launch science-specific versions soon) or you could create your own using a tool such as Microsoft's Forms application.

When asking students to do homework that prepares them for upcoming lessons – often a reading task looking at the background or key foundational knowledge of a topic – you must consider two things. Firstly, how you will assess that the work has been done and, secondly, what you will do about those students who have not completed the task. If this preparation work is crucial to understanding new learning, then making sure that students have understood it must form the first part of your lesson, so a quiz to evaluate the learning from the homework is essential. Spending time going over the key points will scaffold those who haven't completed the homework (and you might have other sanctions to hand to ensure this doesn't happen again).

Further reading

Black, P. and Harrison, C. (2004) *Science Inside the Black Box: Assessment for Learning in the Science Classroom*. Brentford: GL Assessment.

Education Endowment Foundation (2018) *Improving Secondary Science: Guidance report*. Available at: https://educationendowmentfoundation.org. uk/education-evidence/guidance-reports/science-ks3-ks4

Education Endowment Foundation (2020) *Special Educational Needs in Mainstream Schools: Guidance report*. Available at: https:// educationendowmentfoundation.org.uk/education-evidence/guidance-reports/send

Lemov, D. (2015) *Teach Like a Champion 2.0*. Hoboken, NJ: Jossey-Bass.

Rosenshine, B. (2012) 'Principles of instruction: Research-based strategies that all teachers should know'. *American Educator*, 36(1), 12–19.

Sherrington, T. (2017) *The Learning Rainforest*. Woodbridge: John Catt Educational Ltd.

CHAPTER 6
WHAT ARE THE BIG THEMES IN EACH SUBJECT AND HOW DO I TEACH THEM?

Core concepts and big ideas

Big ideas (such as that all matter in the Universe is made of very small particles) recur throughout a student's life engagement with science, constantly being developed and expanded. In contrast, *core concepts* (such as states of matter) form the knowledge associated with a particular topic or area of study. Core concepts are the topics and substantive knowledge that will be taught to put the big ideas into practice.

It is helpful to have an awareness of how core concepts fit into big ideas, as by pointing out these links to students, you can help them to build more complex mental models of the links between different scientific topics. Consider this familiar example. A student comes out of an exam and accusingly says to the teacher, 'There was a question on arctic foxes, but you've never taught us about them!'. The teacher replies, 'But the question was on adaptations to the cold. Don't you remember when we did polar bears and talked about how they were adapted?'. The student failed to connect the example to the principle. The more work teachers do to help students transfer knowledge from the individual example, lesson or topic to the big concepts and ideas, the better our students will become at science.

A great activity for this is to get students routinely mind mapping the big ideas. Give students a blank sheet with a big idea in the middle of the page. Give them time to fill the page with every fact, idea or example that they can connect to this big idea. Then show them your own completed example and ask them – maybe in a different colour – to add the knowledge they have forgotten to include. This is a very visual way of helping students build their schemas, connecting core concepts and examples to big ideas.

What are the big ideas in biology?

Big ideas in biology	Core concepts in biology
Cells	• Different types of cells – animal, plant, bacteria • Genetics and DNA • Functions of parts of a cell and structural adaptations • Biological molecules: lipids, proteins, carbohydrates and nucleic acids • Food testing
Respiration and gas exchange	• Gas exchange in plants • Cellular respiration (anaerobic and aerobic) • Human gas exchange systems
Ecology	• Energy transfer • Different types of producers and consumers • Field work techniques • Food production in an ecosystem • Food webs • Abiotic and biotic factors • The role of microorganisms • Human impact on the environment
Photosynthesis	• Respiration in plants • Nutrition in plants
Health	• Diseases • Pathogens • Immune system • Drugs • Antibiotics • Medicines • Healthy diets
Transport systems	• In plants – e.g. xylem and phloem • In humans – e.g. circulatory system →

Big ideas in biology	Core concepts in biology
Body systems	• The skeletal, digestive, nervous, hormonal, urinary, circulatory and muscular systems • Nutrition
Coordination and control	• Homeostasis • Human nervous and hormonal systems • Hormones in human reproduction
Inheritance	• Heredity • Model of DNA (Crick, Watson and Franklin) • Importance of biodiversity • Continuous and discontinuous variation • Genomes • Sex determination in humans
Evolution	• Natural selection • Evolution – the process and evidence • Ethical implications of modern biotechnology

Example: bringing teaching of plants alive in biology

Teaching about plants underpins many of the big ideas in biology. The topic can be seen by some students as 'dry'; the teacher's job is to consciously try to bring this aspect of the subject alive. Here are some top tips to try:

■ Get students making models.

■ Maximise the use of even seemingly basic practicals – ink travelling up celery can be illustrative and enjoyable for students.

■ Use microscopes as often as possible.

■ Explicitly talk about the wonder and awe you feel – fake it if necessary! – when exploring the world of plants.

What are the big ideas in chemistry?

Big ideas in chemistry	Core concepts in chemistry
All matter in the Universe is made of very small particles	• States of matter • Elements, mixtures and compounds • Atomic structure • The Periodic Table • Rates of reaction • Electrolysis
Properties of substances can be explained in terms of their atomic and molecular structure	• The Periodic Table • Atomic structure • Materials and their properties • Chemical bonding • Electrolysis
Objects can affect other objects at a distance	• Atomic structure • Chemical bonding • Electrolysis
The total amount of energy in the Universe is always the same but can be transferred from one energy store to another during an event	• Exothermic and endothermic reactions • Chemical reactions • Rates of reaction
Atoms, molecules and compounds can react to form new products	• Acid, alkalis, bases and their reactions • The extraction of metals from their ores • The reactions of metals • The formation of salts • Reactions of organic compounds • Rates of reaction →

Big ideas in chemistry	Core concepts in chemistry
The composition of the Earth and its atmosphere and the processes occurring within them shape the Earth's surface and its climate	• Environmental chemistry • The Earth's resources • The Earth and its atmosphere • Water, treatment, rusting and its prevention • The extraction of metals from their ores • Crude oil and its derivatives
Genetic information is passed down from one generation of organisms to another	• The structure of DNA

Example: bringing teaching of the Periodic Table alive in chemistry

The Periodic Table lies at the centre of chemistry teaching. It is a wonder of form and function, showing the relationships between elements and their reactions, but also their underlying atomic and electronic structures. While a science or chemistry teacher sees all this, too often students just see the table as a list of elements. You can help bring the Periodic Table to life for students by looking at the story of its development. The work of John Newlands, Wolfgang Döbereiner, Dmitri Mendeleev and others in finding order in a seemingly random group of elements is a powerful tool to help students engage with the Periodic Table. An excellent documentary that explores this story in full is *Chemistry: a Volatile History – the order of the elements* (episode 2) by Professor Jim Al-Khalili on the BBC.

Another option to bring the Periodic Table to life is through hands-on work, by letting students see and experience the periodicity of the elements. Through practical work and demonstrations, you can show students the reactivity relationships shown in the Periodic Table. You can demonstrate the reactions of the alkali metals, look at the reactivity of the halogens through displacement reactions, juxtapose the properties of the transition metals to those of the more reactive Group 1 and Group 2 metals.

Students often have questions about elements that are not available for use in the classroom. The University of Nottingham's 'Periodic Videos' website (http://www.periodicvideos.com) provides short videos looking at the properties, reactions and uses of *all* elements up to and including oganesson (element 118).

What are the big ideas in physics?

Big ideas in physics	Core concepts in physics
All matter in the Universe is made of very small particles	• Particle model • States of matter • Thermodynamics • Drag forces • Electricity (point charges) • Nuclear model
Objects can affect other objects at a distance	• Forces • Electrostatics • Magnetism • Electromagnetism • Space physics – planetary motion
Changing the movement of an object requires a net force to be acting on it	• Forces and motion • Pressure • Electrostatics • Magnetism • Electromagnetism • Space physics – planetary motion • Motion
The total amount of energy in the Universe is always the same but can be transferred from one energy store to another during an event	• Energy change and transfer • Particle model • States of matter • Space physics – origins of the Universe (steady state theory) • Fuels • Waves and wave motion
Our Solar System is a very small part of one of billions of galaxies in the Universe	• Space physics

Example: bringing teaching about space alive in physics

It is hard to include practical work in teaching space physics, so there is a risk it can become textbook heavy and rather 'dry'. As the teacher, it is your role to share your enthusiasm for the topic. Luckily, there are lots of other ways to bring space alive in the classroom. The exploration of space is regularly in the news, so find news stories to bring to the lesson. Share the big idea of space as the 'final frontier' for modern explorers; celebrate space as an unknown area waiting to be discovered, and scientists at the forefront of this work.

There are lots of inspirational public figures who are experts in space research, and many of them share videos and resources that will enhance your own teaching:

- The YouTube channel of renowned physicist Brian Cox (@profbriancox4431) is stuffed with videos on many of the big questions about space.

- Check out the Instagram of astronaut Tim Peake (@astro_timpeake) for photos from space and insights into the work of astronauts.

- @hubblespacetelescope on YouTube shares the 'grace and beauty of the Universe'.

- @NASA on YouTube has news, science and a whole variety of perspectives on the work of scientists in space exploration today.

- The James Webb telescope website (https://webbtelescope.org/home) has resources, including zoomable imagery, videos, infographics, activities and articles, inspired by the work of the largest, most powerful space telescope ever built.

- The website 'If the moon were a pixel' (https://joshworth.com/dev/pixelspace/pixelspace_solarsystem.html) has an excellent scrollable graphic to help students understand the scale of space.

- The Jim Al-Khalili programme *Secrets of Size: Atoms to Supergalaxies* on the BBC explores the scale of the Universe from tiny atoms to galaxies.

When do I teach big ideas about science?

In *Working With Big Ideas of Science Education*, Harlen *et al.* (2015) set out four key principles students should be taught about science (see Chapter 2, Four big ideas about science):

1 Science is about finding the cause or causes of phenomena in the natural world.

2 Scientific explanations, theories and models are those that best fit the evidence available at a particular time.

3 The knowledge produced by science is used in engineering and technologies to create products to serve human ends.

4 Applications of science often have ethical, social, economic and political implications.

It is helpful to plan specific opportunities within each scientific discipline to address each big idea.

When can I teach big ideas about biology?

There are multiple opportunities during delivery of the biology curriculum to link content back to these central themes.

1 Causes

There are myriad opportunities in biology for teaching about phenomena in the natural world, from cells, to photosynthesis and life processes. Teaching about ecosystems is an opportunity to revisit and deepen student understanding of the causes of phenomena, as organisms and ecosystems are interdependent.

2 Theories

Evolution, including natural selection, is a powerful topic for teaching how scientific models develop over time. Since the topic features in popular culture, students often have their own ideas and perspectives. Exploring student views is not only engaging but provides important opportunities for science teachers to help students understand the evidence behind evolution and how this reflects our best understanding at this time.

3 Engineering and technology

The medical aspects of biology provide fertile ground for discussing the practical real-world applications of the subject. Students are already starting to explore how medicines are developed, and how diseases are spread, controlled and treated. Following Covid, there are contemporary opportunities to talk to students about how scientists have researched and discovered vaccines and sought ways to minimise the impact of disease.

4 Implications

Opportunities to discuss the ethical implications of biology will be found when teaching modern biotechnology, the use of stem cells and gene editing. Engaging and provocative discussions can be had about whether it is ethical to edit conditions such as Huntington's disease out of a child's DNA before birth, and whether there should be limits to gene editing in general – should we be able to edit DNA for eye colour, or sex, for example?

When can I teach big ideas about chemistry?

Here we look at how these big ideas about science can be addressed through chemistry teaching.

1 Causes

Exploring the causes of reactions is a core part of the subject, and thus every time chemical processes are explored, students are exploring causes of phenomena in the natural world.

2 Theories

Examining the evidence about climate change is an excellent opportunity in chemistry to look at how scientific explanations will always be a 'best fit' at a given time.

3 Engineering and technology

Chemistry underpins much of the work of industry today, so there are lots of practical examples teachers can draw on to illustrate applications of the subject. For example, the processes of fractional distillation of crude oil and cracking to make more useful materials are practical examples of technology using chemistry.

Teaching about life cycle assessments and recycling processes is a good opportunity to introduce the environmental impacts of creating products for human use. The exploration of recycling processes is also an opportunity to explore how new chemical technologies are evolving to recycle more types of products.

4 Implications

Exploring the Earth as a source of limited resources and the efficacy of recycling are examples of the social implications of chemistry in action.

The development of chemical weapons from the 20th century onwards is a topic with contemporary relevance as we see the implications of such weapons being used in wars today. This could be explored when teaching the Haber process – and is also a good opportunity for cross-curricular teaching with history.

When can I teach big ideas about physics?

And finally, let's look at how these big ideas about science can be addressed in physics lessons.

1 Causes

In physics, the study of forces and energy provides wonderful opportunities for exploring concrete examples of phenomena in the natural world. Gravity, speed, elastic stretching and pressure are all excellent topics for exploring the physical processes evident in the natural world.

2 Theories

The development of the nuclear model is a good example of the evolution of scientific theory for discussion with students, helping them to understand how the nuclear model has changed over time from an early theory in Ancient Greece – when the original word 'atomos' (meaning indivisible) was described by Democritus as the smallest unit of matter that could be imagined. Centuries later, Dalton proposed that there were different types of atoms, understood as solid spheres. This was thought of as the best explanation until electrons, smaller than atoms, were discovered. The plum pudding model of the atom was proposed, replacing the ball model. Rutherford's gold foil experiment developed the theory further, suggesting atoms contained a nucleus. Bohr put electrons in energy shells around the outside of the atom ... and so scientific thinking can be shown to have developed and responded to the best available evidence at the time.

3 Engineering and technology

When teaching about transformers, teachers can examine how physics powers the home of every student through the National Grid and develop student understanding of the alternating current (AC) supply and its main features. Radio waves, microwaves and x-rays are all examples of substantive knowledge you can teach which allow for exploration of the practical, real-world applications of physics that will be familiar to students in their own lives.

4 Implications

Teaching about radioactive and nuclear materials provides a good time to explore the ethical and political implications of physics. The impact of waste disposal of hazardous materials can be explored and illustrated through case studies such as the Fukushima nuclear power plant disaster, or contemporary concerns about nuclear power plants in the Ukraine–Russia war. Renewable versus non-renewable energy (if pitched as a choice) is a good opportunity for debating the pros and cons of different physics processes and the debate is reflected in our political and economic headlines every day.

Further reading

Harlen, W. (ed.) (2015) *Working With Big Ideas of Science Education.* IAP. Available at: http://www.ase.org.uk/bigideas

CHAPTER 7
HOW DO I BREAK DOWN COMPLEX IDEAS AND MAKE ABSTRACT IDEAS CONCRETE?

There are many moments in science teaching when the skill of the teacher is to help students understand abstract and complex concepts. No one method alone will help students to understand these complex ideas; instead, the best teachers use a mix of methods to help students develop their understanding.

Strategies can include using:

- direct explanations
- lots of examples
- visuals
- analogies and comparisons to real-world experience
- experiential learning, practicals and demonstrations
- connections between abstract and concrete ideas.

In this section, we will explore some important learning points in each of the three sciences and outline a variety of teaching approaches designed to clarify the ideas for students.

Teaching respiration and breathing in biology

The topic of respiration is complex and should be broken down for students. You will need to address common misconceptions, break down a number of complex processes and use a variety of strategies to illustrate those processes before students gain a full understanding. Respiration can be aerobic or anaerobic; this chapter will deal with teaching students about aerobic respiration and breathing.

Misconceptions

A common misconception to be addressed is that respiration is breathing, or that breathing is respiration, rather than the processes being distinct from one another. Teaching should explicitly address this misconception at all points.

The equation for respiration is:

$$\text{glucose} + \text{oxygen} \rightarrow \text{water} + \text{carbon dioxide} \;(+ \text{energy})$$

When teaching this chemical reaction, take care with the language you use. Saying 'plus energy' when writing the equation on the board might reinforce a misconception that respiration *creates* energy, as opposed to energy being *released*. This is because students often interpret 'plus' as 'producing'. A simple strategy is just to point out the misconception as you write the equation.

Plant respiration is also ripe for misconceptions. Students often forget respiration happens in plants, due to the misapprehension that breathing and respiration are the same. Be prepared to head off queries about whether plants can breathe by reiterating the difference between breathing and respiration.

Direct explanation

Direct explanation from the teacher helps counter misconceptions and gives students a rigorous basis for grasping the core concepts. Be sure to define concepts:

- **Breathing** is the exchange of gases, the movement of gases into and out of the body; the taking in of oxygen and giving out of carbon dioxide. Breathing takes place in the lungs.
- **Respiration** is the reaction of oxygen with glucose to form carbon dioxide and water, a biochemical process. Respiration is the chemical process by which organic compounds release energy. Respiration takes place in the mitochondria of cells all over the body.

When teaching this topic, expect to put a lot of effort into ensuring that students realise these are distinct and individual processes. Plan your lessons accordingly. Be clear that respiration is a chemical process. Share with students the chemical reaction and balanced formula, and state that during this reaction, chemical energy is converted to other forms of energy that the body can use. Stressing the idea that energy is *released* rather than made is crucial; 'production' of energy is a common misconception.

It is also important to link the two different concepts. When teaching respiration, point out that it requires oxygen. How did this oxygen get into the cells? Discuss how it flows through the blood to get to the cells. How did it get into the blood? It was absorbed into the blood in the lungs through breathing. A similar discussion centres around the removal of carbon dioxide. Make it clear that respiration is the *reaction*; breathing is the *mechanism* that provides oxygen for respiration and removes the carbon dioxide produced by respiration.

You can also look at examples of texts – adapted from news articles, taken from textbooks or from student work. Display the text on the board and analyse the use of the terms 'breathing' and 'respiration'. Are they being used correctly? If not, why not?

Using visuals

Breathing – the action of the lungs and diaphragm to draw air in and out of the body – can be modelled using a bell jar with balloons acting as the lungs and a stretched piece of flexible plastic across the bottom of the jar for the diaphragm. By manipulating the diaphragm, you can show air moving in and out of the lungs. This demonstration can be combined with an activity asking students to think about their own bodies and the contrast with the bell jar model. Ask students to feel their rib cage as they breathe in and out. Can they see how the bell jar model is different from their body? (Hint: the human rib cage moves, while the walls of the bell jar are fixed.)

This demonstration of breathing in action can be presented alongside diagrams showing the true structure of the lungs, allowing students to see that lungs aren't balloons but consist of a detailed structure, including the trachea, bronchi, bronchioles and alveoli.

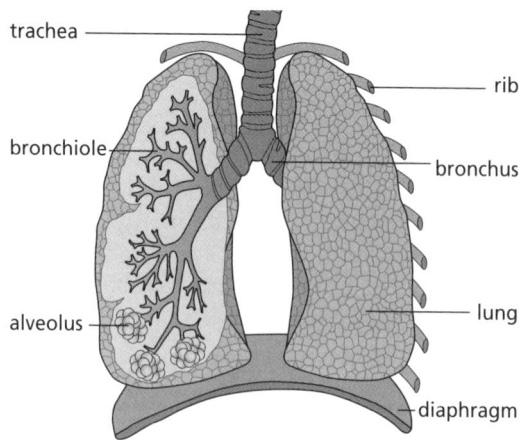

▲ Figure 4 The structure of the lungs

When using a diagram like Figure 4, start with the trachea, describing it as the main route for gases to move in and out of the lungs. As shown in the figure, the trachea is ridged with loops of cartilage to help keep it open at all times. Students should be able to locate their own trachea in their necks and feel the ridges caused by the loops of cartilage for themselves. From here, you can describe the branching nature of the pathway that gases take into the lungs. The branches get smaller and smaller, moving through the bronchial tree down to the alveoli.

Introduce a diagram, such as that in Figure 5, showing the structure of an alveolus. Point out how the capillary loops round the alveolus. Show the exchange of the two gases, carbon dioxide and oxygen, using arrows in and out of the alveolus.

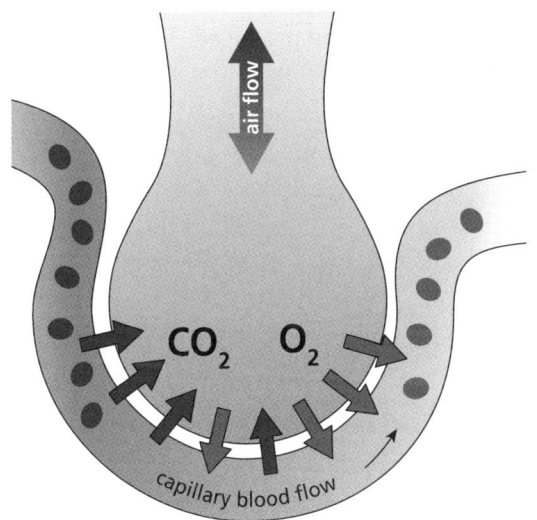

▲ Figure 5 The structure of an alveolus

Diagrams of the structure of the lungs, like Figures 4 and 5, serve as a strong starting point for performing a lung dissection (see page 95). While performing this dissection, referring to diagrams such as the ones displayed here can help students to identify the parts of the lungs. For respiration, treat the equation as a visual, using it to help students build an image of the process. Share a visual such as the one in Figure 6.

$$C_6H_{12}O_6 + 6O_2 \longrightarrow 6CO_2 + 6H_2O$$

glucose   +   oxygen   carbon   +   water   +   (energy)
                                       dioxide

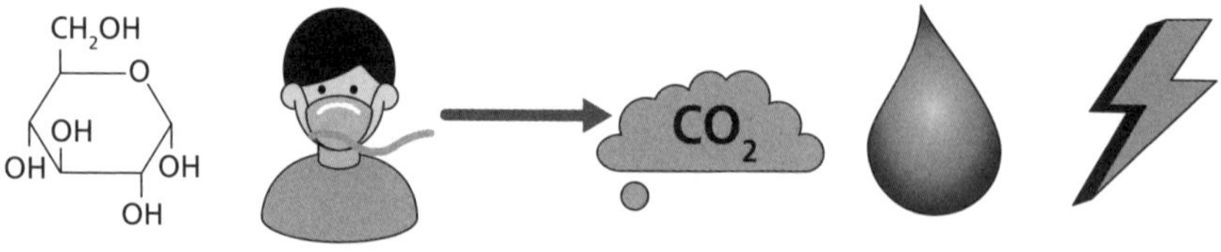

▲ Figure 6 The respiration process

Point out where the oxygen comes from (breathing) and where the carbon dioxide goes. You can also look at how individual cells gain this oxygen and get rid of the carbon dioxide produced. The diagram in Figure 7 can be contrasted with the gas exchange in the alveolus (Figure 5).

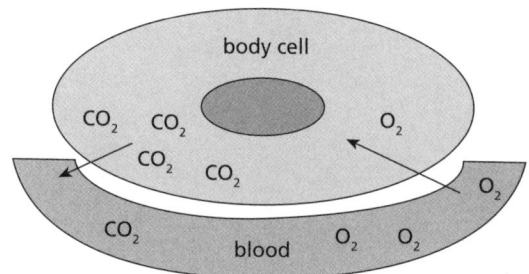

▲ Figure 7 Gas exchange in individual cells

By looking at a diagram of a cell, you can show students where respiration happens: in the mitochondria of the cell. Contrast this with the location of gas exchange and breathing. A simple table can help clarify the difference between respiration and breathing:

Process	Where it happens	Outcome
Respiration	Mitochondria in cells	To provide energy
Breathing	Alveoli in the lungs	Gas exchange

Practicals as experiential learning

Practicals can provide students with a strong experience that allows them to relate what they see to the abstract knowledge they have learned through diagrams and equations. The respiration topic provides opportunities to reinforce learning through a lung dissection and using the 'huff and puff' experiment.

Lung dissection

Equipment

- Lungs or plucks (if students are carrying out the practical, you will need one lung per group; if you are demonstrating, one set of lungs will be sufficient)

- Scalpels

- Dissecting scissors

- Rubber tubing

- Foot or hand pump

- Tray

- Latex gloves (nitrile gloves for those who have latex allergies)

- Camera to display your demonstration

- Balance or scale to find the mass of the lungs and tape measure to find the dimensions

- Transparent plastic bag large enough to accommodate the lungs

Setting up the practical

Lungs for the dissection can be obtained from a butcher or specialist school science supplier. Lungs obtained from a butcher can often be damaged during the butchery process or cut into as part of the examination of the butchered animal. Discussion with your butcher beforehand can help you obtain lungs of a suitable quality for the purpose of this experiment. Some butchers will be able to provide plucks rather than just lungs. Plucks are lungs with the heart and the major connecting blood vessels. These can enable students to explore the connection between the heart and the lungs.

If doing the practical as a demonstration only, one tray with lungs and dissection equipment is all that is needed. If students are going to carry out the dissection, then have your technician provide one tray per group with all the relevant material.

Before the practical, consider that some students may have issues carrying out animal dissection due to ethical or religious reasons. Accommodate them in the class as best as possible; consider using videos, textbooks or other multimedia approaches for them to experience the practical.

Teacher in action

Demonstrate exactly what the students are looking for during this dissection, guiding them through the steps and pointing out the key structures and how to find them. It is useful for students to see this being done before attempting it themselves. Depending on the set up of the lab, using a camera to project the dissection onto the board may make it easier for all students to see clearly.

First, look at the lungs as a whole, comparing them to a diagram (see Figure 4 on page 92). Show the students some of the key external features, for instance the trachea. You may be able to highlight the ridges of cartilage on the outside of the trachea, asking students why these are here. Next you should measure the lungs, approximate their volume and weigh them. This can give students context for the size of these organs within the body. Now you can start to explore more of the structure of the lungs. You should seek to identify and show students the following structures within the lungs:

1 the bronchi, and how these diverge from the trachea, delivering air to the left and right lungs

2 arteries and veins linking the heart to the lungs; highlight the thinner vein walls compared to artery walls

3 the structure of the trachea, and the ridges of cartilage around it

4 the point at which a bronchus first splits to form bronchioles

5 the membrane covering the lungs (the pleural membrane)

6 the larynx.

Then, demonstrate the lung in action. If the larynx is still attached to the trachea, demonstrate the movement of air through the larynx by squeezing it. Explore the lung tissue. Cut a small piece of the lung tissue away, show its spongy texture, and drop it into water to demonstrate the low density of lung tissue even when not inflated. Lastly, you can attempt to inflate the lungs by inserting a piece of rubber tubing into the trachea and attaching it to a pump. Place the lungs into a transparent plastic bag to ensure no liquid is sprayed across the room by the inflation. Use the pump to inflate the lungs, showing students how they increase in size. Do not be tempted to breathe into the tube to inflate the lungs; you are likely to get a mouthful of very horrid air come back to you.

As you demonstrate, use three key questions:

1 Why are the vein walls thinner than the artery walls?

 Answer: the pressure is greater in the arteries.

2 Why does the piece of lung placed in water float?

 Answer: it has lots of small alveoli or air sacs.

3 Why shouldn't I blow into the lung myself?

 Answer: lungs are quite elastic, so when I stop blowing in, they will push the air back down the tube.

Finally, demonstrate to the students how to clean up after such a dissection. Make sure all of the lung material is back on the tray, wipe down all surfaces using disinfectant, remove your gloves and place them into the bin before washing your hands with soap and warm water.

Students in action

Students can now work their way through the dissection, repeating the steps that have been shown to them in the demonstration. Prompt these steps by displaying the following instructions:

1 Describe the look, feel and colour of the lungs.

2 Identify the trachea and explore the texture of its wall.

3 Explore the tubes that enter the lungs and see how they divide.

4 Identify any membrane surrounding the lungs.

5 Inflate the lungs (following your teacher's instructions) and observe how they behave.

6 Cut a piece of lung tissue and observe the cut surface and how the tissue behaves when you drop it into water.

While students do this, move around the room, supporting them in their work, showing them how to use their equipment and pointing out the next steps they need to take. Be mindful as you move around the room that students can often be squeamish about handling or cutting into the lungs and encourage them to do so.

You must also be very mindful of the dangers present in this practical; students will be using scalpels which are sharp and dangerous if used incorrectly. Ensure that you remain vigilant while students are working. Choose a position in the room where you can easily observe the students.

When helping or talking to a group of students, ensure that you are scanning the room at regular intervals to check that other groups are maintaining the standards you require.

Learning from practicals in action
Students should gain a greater understanding of the structure of the lungs and be able to link these structures to their functions, such as knowing why the trachea has cartilage ridges in it, and why lung tissue is spongy and has a low density. This experiment is also a key experiential learning moment – it will help students make links between what they see in a textbook, presentation or diagram and the real world. It will make their learning concrete.

The 'huff and puff' experiment

Another practical connected to respiration is the 'huff and puff' experiment. Students will analyse the gas they breathe in and out to show that exhaled air contains more carbon dioxide than inhaled air. This simple 'huff and puff' experiment can be performed using the equipment setup in Figure 8.

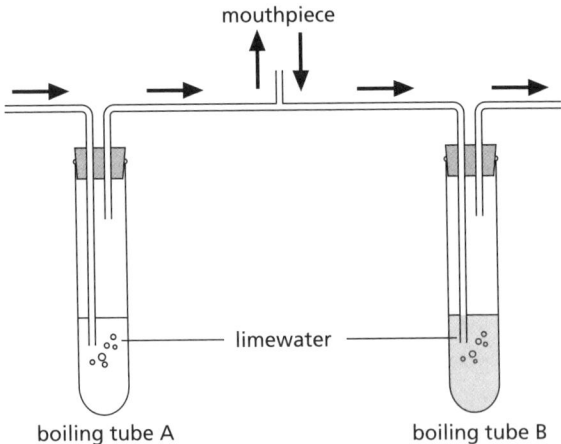

▲ Figure 8 The 'huff and puff' experiment

Students breathe in and out through the mouthpiece in the centre. As they breathe in, gas is drawn in through tube A, bubbling through the limewater, and as they breathe out, gas is expelled through tube B, again bubbling through limewater as it does so.

The exhaled air contains about 100 times more carbon dioxide than inhaled air (about 0.04% in inhaled air compared to about 4% in exhaled air) and so students should observe the limewater on side B become cloudy much sooner than that on side A.

When students analyse their results for the 'huff and puff' experiment, try to guide their thinking with a series of questions:

1 Which side, A or B, was bubbling when you inhaled?

2 Which side, A or B, was bubbling when you exhaled?

3 Which side, A or B, went cloudy quickest?

4 What does your answer to question three tell you about the amount of carbon dioxide bubbling through this side of the experiment?

5 Which gas, the inhaled or exhaled, contained more carbon dioxide? How do your results support this?

The 'huff and puff' experiment could also be carried out using carbon dioxide and oxygen gas sensors if these are available.

Allowing students to measure their own lung capacity and function with spirometers and peak flow meters can help them to make sense of what they have learned about the structure and functions of lungs, and how this relates to them personally. You could contrast their lung capacity and peak flow with that of professional athletes and also show how athletes have their breathing analysed (for example, by showing a video of a VO_2 max test).

Analogies

Analogies and models can be useful in describing structures within the human body, allowing students to make sense of a complex structure by relating it to something that they recognise, and making its composition and function easier to understand. For example, the lungs can be modelled as balloons within a bell jar. The way capillaries wrap around cells in order to deliver oxygen and remove carbon dioxide can be modelled using oranges in their plastic net bag. The oranges represent the cells, with the plastic netting representing the surrounding capillaries. There are other possible analogies, but it is key that students use them to further their understanding and not fully equate the model or analogy with the actual thing. Lungs are not balloons – being much more complicated in reality – but the analogy can help students to see how simple elements of the lungs work.

Teaching photosynthesis in biology

Photosynthesis is an important area of study in biology. Understanding the reaction itself, the conditions it requires, and how plant leaves are adapted for photosynthesis are all key learning points for this topic.

Direct explanation and examples

A direct explanation of photosynthesis begins by addressing the question, 'where do plants get their food from?'. The answer is that plants can make their own food in the form of glucose, which is then normally stored in the plant as starch.

Then introduce the word and symbol equations for the reaction.

$$\text{carbon dioxide} + \text{water} \rightarrow \text{glucose} + \text{oxygen}$$

$$6CO_2 + 6H_2O \rightarrow C_6H_{12}O_6 + 6O_2$$

Tell students that plants get carbon dioxide from the air and water through their roots. However, also point out that just adding these two things together will not result in glucose being made; special conditions are needed for this reaction to occur. These conditions are sunlight and the presence of chlorophyll. State that sunlight provides the energy needed for the reaction to happen (you could link this to the idea of an endothermic reaction from chemistry) and that chlorophyll is a green pigment present in certain parts of plant cells (chloroplasts) that can absorb sunlight and use it to make glucose.

Finally, examine diagrams of plant cells and discuss *where* in the cell the reaction takes place. This can then be extended by looking at cross sections through a leaf and at the surface of a leaf, exploring how it is adapted to maximise the amount of photosynthesis that can take place. The key here is that the direct instruction should show the students *what* is happening and *where* it is taking place.

Using visuals

Diagrams showing where photosynthesis takes place are a useful aid to this topic. Start with a plant cell showing the chloroplasts (Figure 9). This can act as a seed for a discussion about the process of photosynthesis and why chlorophyll is green.

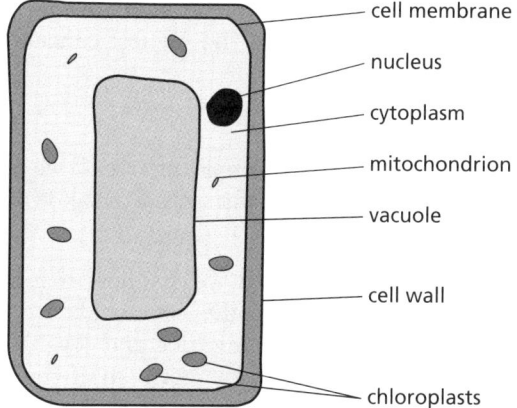

▲ Figure 9 The structure of a plant cell

A diagram showing the structure of a leaf (Figure 10) could also be used to illustrate that stomata are present on the surface of the leaf. This allows for gaseous exchange, which could be contrasted with breathing in humans.

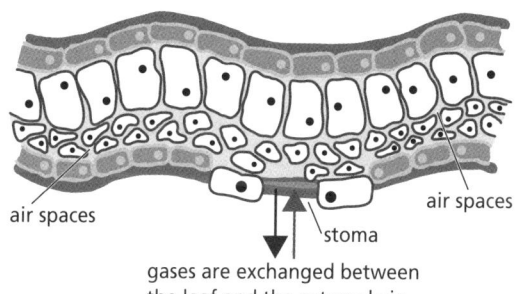

air spaces

air spaces

stoma

gases are exchanged between the leaf and the external air

▲ Figure 10 A cross section of a leaf

Practicals as experiential learning

Practical work allows students to connect the abstract knowledge they have learned to their real experiences.

Examining leaves under a microscope

Microscope practical work offers an excellent opportunity for students to see the structure of a leaf and a plant cell. They can make their own impressions of the top and bottom surface of a leaf using nail polish and then examine these under the microscope, looking for the presence of stomata. Students can also look at cross sections of leaves (slides should be provided). They can again observe the stomata and work out how they allow air into the leaf, and find the highest concentration of cells containing chlorophyll.

Testing plants for starch

By getting students to perform a simple practical, we can show that plants produce their own food in the form of starch and that they require sunlight to do so.

To test a leaf to see if it contains starch, we first need to remove the green colouring (the chlorophyll). To do this, the leaf must be heated in ethanol. Place the leaf to be tested into a boiling tube and cover it with ethanol. Then place this boiling tube into a hot water bath (if you have access to an electrically heated water bath, set it to between 80 and 90°C, otherwise use boiling water from a kettle in a beaker and place the boiling tube into the beaker). After about 5 minutes, the green colouring of the leaf should have dissolved into the ethanol. Remove the leaf, rinse it with water and then place it into a petri dish. Use a dropping bottle to add iodine solution to the leaf. The presence of starch in the leaf makes the iodine turn a deep blue–black colour, showing that photosynthesis has been taking place in the leaf.

In this experiment, you could use leaves from two different plants: one that has spent the last 48 hours in an area where it will get access to lots of light and one that has been placed in a dark cupboard. Students should be able to see starch present in the one that has had access to light but not in the one that has been away from it, highlighting the need for light as a crucial part of photosynthesis.

Using algae balls to investigate photosynthesis

Algae, in the form of immobilised balls, can be used to investigate the conditions needed for photosynthesis. These balls can be placed in a simple hydrogencarbonate indicator solution, so that when they photosynthesise, the indicator will change colour. Different investigations could be completed by students:

■ changing the light intensity (by moving the light source nearer or further from the algae balls)

■ changing the frequency of the light (with coloured filters between the lamp and the algae)

■ comparing algae that have been in the presence of light with some that have not.

It should be noted that results from this experiment can take some time. Make sure you have some clearly displayed examples of the indicator colours at different pHs for the students to use as a reference during the practical work.

Teaching atoms, molecules, elements and compounds in chemistry

Atoms, molecules, elements and compounds is a fundamental topic in chemistry that recurs in the curriculum throughout secondary school and into further study.

Direct explanation and examples

In order for our students to understand the difference between an atom, an element and a compound, we need to explain their definitions deliberately, highlighting the differences between these related ideas.

Start with the atom. Begin by asking the question, 'what is an atom?'. Answers like 'it is a really small bit of stuff' reflect a vague awareness of the concept. The teacher should then provide a scientifically precise definition: an atom is the smallest piece of something that is chemically active.

Now we need to give definitions and examples of elements, molecules, compounds and mixtures:

- We can state that the elements are the 100+ different types of atoms that are listed in the Periodic Table. We could show some examples of elements: a piece of magnesium ribbon, a block of iron and some sulfur, for example. Emphasise that there is only one type of atom in these substances and so they are elements.

- Next, look at molecules, stating that they are two or more atoms bonded together into a linked group. A bonded group of atoms is a molecule. Then look at diagrams of different molecules. Some should contain only one type of atom: point out that these are elements *and* molecules. Others should contain more than one type of atom within the molecule.

- Now, we can introduce the definition of a compound: two or more types of atoms bonded together. Give examples of compounds such as water and carbon dioxide, and show diagrams of what the bonded atoms would look like if we could see them. Point out how compounds differ from elements, but also that compounds are a form of molecule.

- Finally, we can introduce the idea of a mixture. In a mixture, we have more than one type of particle present in the same space. A mixture could contain elements, compounds or both; point this out and share some examples. For instance, when you dissolve sugar into water, you create a liquid that contains both water molecules and sugar molecules mingled together. This is a mixture: different types of particles – atoms or molecules – that are not bonded together and that can, by a simple process, be separated. This should be contrasted with compounds, that contain different atoms bonded together so they cannot be separated easily.

By giving clear, concise definitions of the terms 'atom', 'element', 'molecule', 'compound' and 'mixture', and supporting these with examples, fundamental concepts are made clear to the students.

Using visuals

As students can't see the atoms that make up elements, molecules and compounds, we need to use clear diagrams showing the differences. Simple diagrams showing atoms as spheres, with different elements represented by different colours, can be powerful in reinforcing the definitions.

Figure 11 is a set of diagrams showing elements, compounds and mixtures.

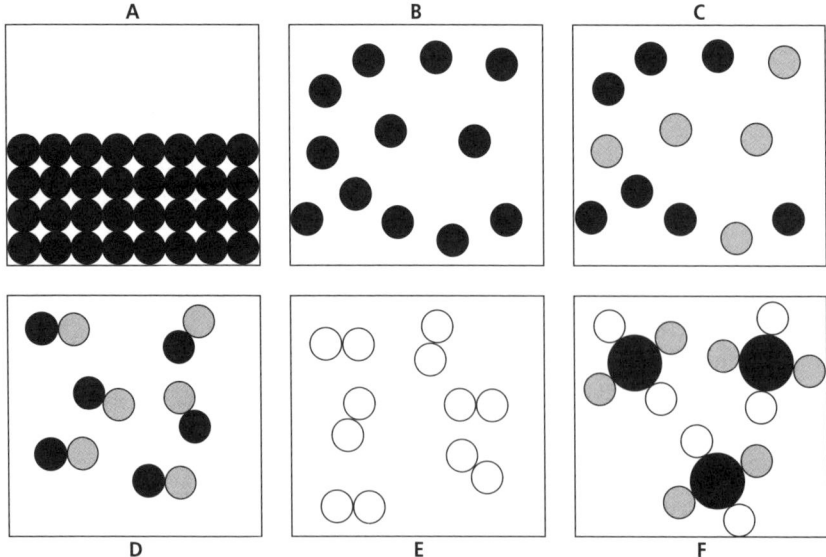

▲ Figure 11 Elements, compounds and mixtures

Display these diagrams on the projector or on a worksheet and ask 'which diagrams show an element?'. Start by modelling your thinking, referring back to the definitions you have taught the students.

Teacher: I know that an element only contains one type of atom. Diagram A only has one type, so that is an element. Diagrams B and E also contain only one type of atom, so they must be elements too. The other diagrams aren't elements as they contain more than one type of atom. For instance, C contains two types of atoms (black and grey), so that can't be an element.

Now ask a series of different questions of students, always prompting them to explain their answers:

Teacher: Which diagram shows atoms forming molecules, but is also an element?

Student: I think it's diagram E.

Teacher: Okay, so how do you know it's an element?

Student: It's only got one type of atom – all the atoms are white.

Teacher: Yes, I agree it's an element, but how do you know it has formed molecules?

Student: Because the white atoms are joined together.

Teacher: What is the word we use to describe atoms that have joined together?

Student: Bonded, the atoms are bonded together to form molecules.

Practicals as experiential learning

Students can't see the atoms and molecules that make up elements and compounds, but they can get hands-on experience of different elements and their properties, and they can examine how some of these elements react to form compounds with different properties.

Demonstration: splitting a compound into its elements using water as an example

Most students will know that water is made up of hydrogen and oxygen, and they are likely to know its chemical formula. We can show them how different the atoms as elements are from the compound by looking at some samples of water, hydrogen and oxygen.

We can also demonstrate that water can be broken down into its elements. Using a Hofmann voltameter, you can show that by running electricity through water, it is possible to break the compound into its elements. Collect the hydrogen and oxygen that form, point out that you have collected twice the volume of hydrogen as oxygen and show the formula of water. Demonstrate that the gases you have collected are indeed what you say they are, by performing the squeaky pop test and the glowing splint test.

You may also be able to follow up on the squeaky pop test. When you do this test, condensation may form on the inside of the boiling tube. Show this condensation to the students and ask them where the water came from. Ask them what they think the hydrogen reacted with (the oxygen in the air). What do you get if you react hydrogen and oxygen together? Water! This reaction is demonstrated by the condensation on the inside of the tube: the original proof that water is not an element.

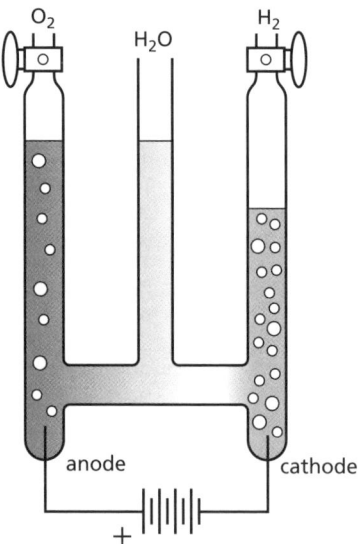

▲ Figure 12 Breaking down water into its elements with a Hofmann voltameter

Demonstration: adding elements together to form a compound

You can illustrate the difference between elements and the compounds they make by demonstrating a reaction between sodium and chlorine. Ask your technician to prepare a gas jar of chlorine with a lid, a brick, a Bunsen burner and some sodium. To safely perform this demonstration, you will need a heat-resistant mat, forceps, a sharp knife, a safe surface on which to cut the sodium and a paper towel.

Leave the chlorine jar and the brick on the heat-resistant mat in a fume cupboard for the demonstration. Students and demonstrator should all wear goggles. Show the students the chlorine and the sodium. Tell them they are elements and review the properties of each. Next, slice off a 6–8 mm cube of sodium. Point out that sodium is soft and has lustre where it has been cut. Wipe the oil from the surface of the sodium with a paper towel. Place the sodium on the brick using the forceps and heat it with the air hole open on the Bunsen burner until it first melts, then catches fire. Once it catches fire, take the lid off the gas jar of chlorine and place it over the sodium. You should see a vigorous reaction and be left at the end with a white cloudy smoke: sodium chloride. Now you can discuss the compound that formed, its properties and how it is different from the elements it is made from. End by using the diagrams in Figure 13 to discuss what the atoms and molecules might look like in the elements and the compound. (Have the students add labels to the diagrams.)

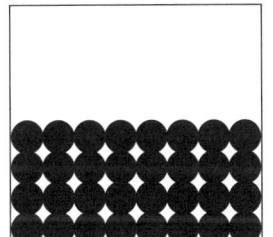 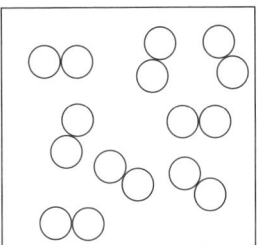 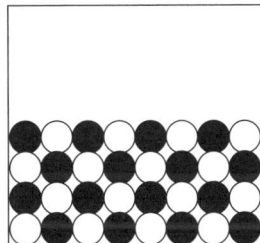

▲ Figure 13 Adding elements together to form a compound

Class practical: reacting iron and sulfur to make iron sulfide

Students can explore the difference between elements and the compounds they form by looking at the reaction between iron and sulfur. To do this as a class practical, each group of students will need a prepared ignition tube, a Bunsen burner, a heat-resistant mat, a small magnet and test-tube tongs. All students and the teacher should wear goggles throughout. Start with the individual elements, iron and sulfur, and describe their properties. Mix small amounts of the elements together and get the students to use a magnet to test the mixture and identify that the elemental iron is magnetic and can be separated from the sulfur due to this property. Then, students heat a pre-prepared mixture of the reactants in an ignition tube. They should hold the tube to the Bunsen burner using the tongs, heat the reactants until they just start to glow, then turn the Bunsen burner off. Once the reaction is complete and the ignition tubes have cooled on the heat-resistant mats, students can observe the properties of the compound that formed.

The easiest change in property for students to observe is that elemental iron is magnetic but that the iron sulfide which forms is not. Students can demonstrate this using the magnets. You can make the key point about the difference between mixtures and compounds; mixtures can be easily separated (in this case, using a magnet to remove the iron), while compounds cannot. Again, follow up the learning from the practical with diagrams representing the atoms and molecules, as in Figure 14.

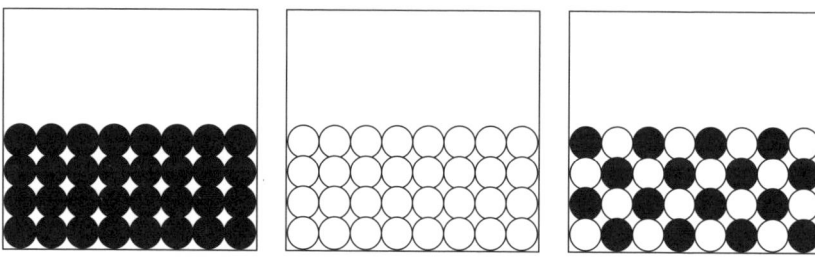

▲ Figure 14 The structure of atoms in iron, sulfur and iron sulfide

Teaching energy change in chemistry

Students need to gain an understanding that when chemical reactions happen, energy can either be taken in (endothermic) or released (exothermic). Also, chemical reactions – be they exothermic or endothermic – require activation energy in order to begin. Here we will look at some examples of strategies to use when teaching this topic.

Direct explanation and examples

Be very clear about the definitions involved in energy change, telling students the facts you expect them to understand, before linking these to concrete real-world examples and students' own hands-on evidence. Start with a demonstration of a reaction that gets visibly hot, setting a fuel on fire for example, and ask students to describe what has happened. Students will – maybe with a little bit of guidance – eventually get to the idea that heat has been given out.

Now, tell students that when chemical reactions happen, energy can be taken in or given out. If energy is given out, this energy is released as heat and makes things hotter, but if energy is taken in, then it removes heat energy from the surroundings, making them colder. There is a common misconception to address here, as students may think that if energy is taken in then things should get hotter as they have more energy: a discussion of the different types of energy (for example, heat, chemical and potential energy) may help avoid this misconception.

Having established the underlying idea, move on to definitions and scientific vocabulary. Give a definition for an exothermic reaction: a reaction that gives out heat energy, making the temperature of the surroundings increase. Explore how this word has been formed: *exo–* meaning *from* or *out of*, and *–thermic* meaning *heat* come together to give us this word that describes this type of reaction.

Then, introduce the definition of an endothermic reaction: a reaction that takes in heat energy. Again, point out how the word is formed using the prefix *endo–* meaning *into*. Now, give the students a number of examples from the real world, such as ice packs from first aid. Students can be asked if they know any examples of exothermic or endothermic reactions. They tend to be able to come up with lots of exothermic reactions but not many endothermic ones; the most student-friendly, real-world example used to be the cooling sensation of eating sherbet, but alas sherbet is not widely consumed by students these days!

We also want students to understand that to *start* a chemical reaction, an energy input is required. Go back to your demonstration of a fuel burning. Why doesn't the fuel combust straight away? Because we need to put some energy in first. This is called activation energy. When burning a fuel in the demonstration, activation energy is provided by the fire from the burning splint used to light it. Give a definition of activation energy to the students: the minimum energy needed for a chemical reaction to happen. Introduce the symbol for activation energy: EA or E_a.

Finally, bring these ideas together in the form of an energy profile diagram, showing students the activation energy change and the overall energy change. Discuss what the diagrams for exothermic and endothermic reactions look like (for example Figure 15).

Using visuals

A key visual for learning is seeing reactions that get hotter and colder. We will explore these in the next section on experiential learning. Here we will focus on the representation of energy change during a reaction, the energy profile diagram.

An energy profile diagram allows a clear view of how the energy changes during a chemical reaction. A student who can draw an energy profile diagram, label it correctly and interpret from the graph whether there is an exothermic or endothermic reaction going on has a good understanding of this topic.

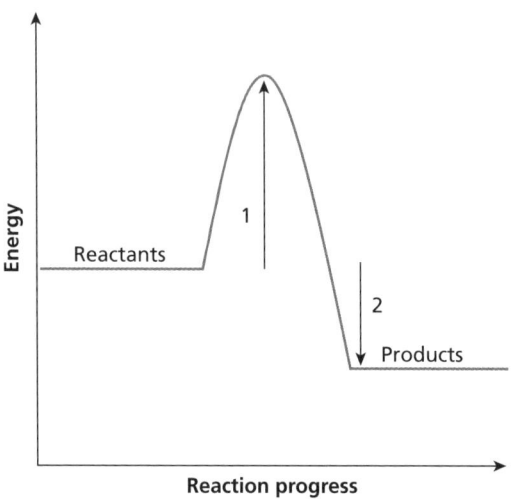

▲ Figure 15 An energy profile diagram for an exothermic reaction

In Figure 15, we can see an energy profile for an exothermic reaction. Showing this to students and explaining its shape facilitates an explanation of how the energy changes as the reaction unfolds. It allows for a clear understanding of both the overall energy change and activation energy.

The crucial part to explain is the significance of the arrows 1 and 2. Arrow 1 represents the activation energy, a term we have already defined to the students. It is the energy we need to put in to make the reaction start. Going back to lighting a fuel, this is the match or spark that starts it off. Unless we give the reactants this energy, they cannot react.

Arrow 2 represents overall energy change (ΔH), the change in energy from the reactants to the products. You can point out how we put in a lot of activation energy, but that is given back as we fall down the other side of the curve, and then we get some extra energy given out. This represents the energy change.

Now, we need to think more about arrow 2 – the extra energy that is given out from the reaction. What happens to it? Point out to the students that it is not *lost*, it is just converted from the chemical energy found in the reactants into another form, heat energy. This energy increases the temperature of the surroundings, making our reaction an exothermic reaction.

Another key point is the direction of the arrows. The arrow for activation energy should point up to the top of the peak. The direction of the energy change arrow is from the level of the reactants to the level of the products, meaning it points down in this case and so the energy change is negative. A negative energy change represents an exothermic reaction.

The diagram in Figure 15 can be compared and contrasted to the reaction profile of an endothermic reaction.

Practicals as experiential learning

The energy change topic in chemistry provides opportunities to reinforce student learning through practicals comparing endothermic and exothermic reactions and burning foodstuffs to compare their energy content.

Comparing endothermic and exothermic reactions

In this experiment, ask students to complete a series of small test-tube reactions and measure the temperature before and after to decide whether the reactions are exothermic or endothermic. The selected reactions should be simple and easy for students to do. Examples include:

1 some neutralisations reactions, e.g. sodium hydroxide and hydrochloric acid

2 a displacement reaction, e.g. copper sulfate and powdered magnesium

3 the reaction of a metal with an acid, e.g. magnesium and hydrochloric acid

While most reactions are exothermic in nature, make sure to include some endothermic reactions. A common endothermic reaction to give to students is the reaction of citric acid and sodium hydrogen carbonate.

Equipment and reagents
- Spatulas
- Thermometers (in the 0 to 110°C range and accurate to 1°C)
- Polystyrene cups

- 250 cm³ beakers
- Measuring cylinders suitable for measuring 10 cm³ of solutions
- Copper sulfate solution (about 0.4 mol dm⁻³)
- Sodium hydroxide solution (about 0.4 mol dm⁻³)
- Sodium hydrogen carbonate solution (about 0.4 mol dm⁻³)
- Sulfuric acid (about 0.4 mol dm⁻³)
- Hydrochloric acid (about 0.4 mol dm⁻³)
- Citric acid (solid)
- Magnesium (powdered)
- Magnesium ribbon (cut into strips about 3–4 cm in length)

A full risk assessment should be done before the experiment takes place. Many of these chemicals are irritants and/or corrosive. Appropriate health and safety measures should be in place before using them in the classroom.

Setting up the practical

Consider how students are going to access the resources. It might be that each group of students can be given individual containers of each solution and solid, or they might need to go and collect these things from a central supply. If the latter, consider how you can avoid congestion around the equipment; perhaps each group nominates one member to collect equipment, or just have a few groups collect equipment at one time.

Give students a copy of the method (from page 116) and allow them time to read it through. To support students with the literacy demands of the method, you could read the method aloud, asking questions to check understanding as you go. Questions to check that students understand the key steps for the experiment include:

- What is the first reaction you are going to do?
- How much sulfuric acid do we measure out?
- How much citric acid do we measure out?
- What do we do with the solutions at the end of the reaction?
- When do we measure the temperature?
- What safety measures will you take during this experiment?

Provide students with a copy of the results table, or instruct them to copy it down.

Reactants	Initial temperature / °C	Final temperature / °C	Temperature change / °C	Exothermic or endothermic
Sodium hydrogen carbonate and citric acid				
Sodium hydroxide and hydrochloric acid				
Copper sulfate and magnesium				
Sulfuric acid and magnesium ribbon				

Teacher in action

First, model how to carry out the experiment using the reaction of sodium hydrogen carbonate and citric acid. As you go, ask the students to help you narrate the process, referring to the method they have in front of them. Use the following questions and answers to check student understanding of the method as you demonstrate the practical:

- What should we do first?

  Answer: place the polystyrene cup into the 250 cm³ beaker.

- Why are we doing this experiment in a polystyrene cup?

  Answer: so that it is insulated from the surroundings and won't lose heat energy.

- How much sodium hydrogen carbonate solution are we using?

  Answer: 10 cm³

  Demonstrate measuring out 10 cm³ sodium hydrogen carbonate solution using a measuring cylinder and pour it into the polystyrene cup.

- What do we do next?

  Answer: measure and record the temperature of the solution.

  Demonstrate measuring the temperature of the solution. Record the result in the results table.

- What do we do next?

  Answer: add the citric acid.

- How much?

  Answer: 4 spatula measures.

  Add the required amount of citric acid to the polystyrene cup.

- What do we do next?

  Answer: stir the solution and measure the temperature of the solution again; record it in the results table.

- Has this been an exothermic or endothermic reaction?

  Answer: endothermic.

- How do you know?

  Answer: the temperature decreased.

Ask a few questions to support students to think metacognitively about their ability to monitor their work independently:

- How long do you think each reaction should take approximately?

  Keeping an eye on the time will help all students complete the experiment roughly together.

- What roles will you have in the group, so that you can work effectively together?

  Having designated roles is an important group work skill and will help the experiments run smoothly.

- What might go wrong with this experiment, and what will you do if that happens?

  Students might measure too much solution, which would mean the temperature change will be lower. As the result is qualitative, the magnitude of change will be less important than whether the temperature increases or decreases. Making sure that students know what to do if something goes wrong will help if they spill a solution or break a piece of equipment.

- What can you do if you get stuck?

  Remind students that they have the written method and their peers for support before they need to turn to the teacher.

After demonstrating the first reaction, tell the students that they are going to complete all four reactions. Their goal is to determine whether each reaction is exothermic or endothermic. Guide the students in safely collecting the equipment needed, bearing in mind the layout of the room and the way in which your technicians have provided the equipment. While students carry out the practical, you should support the groups in carrying out the work and keep them on task. Stand in a position where the entire class is easily visible, so you can spot those students who might need some focused support during the practical. Concentrate your support on ensuring students are following the instructions with scientific precision and in a safe manner.

Students in action

Students should follow the instructions laid out below to carry out the four reactions.

Sodium hydrogen carbonate and citric acid

1 Place the polystyrene cup inside the beaker.

2 Using the measuring cylinder, measure out 10 cm^3 of the sodium hydrogen carbonate solution.

3 Add the sodium hydrogen carbonate solution to the polystyrene cup.

4 Measure the temperature of the sodium hydrogen carbonate solution using the thermometer and record this into your results table.

5 Add 4 spatula measures of citric acid to the polystyrene cup. Stir with the thermometer and record the temperature after mixing into your results table.

6 Work out the temperature change and, hence, whether the reaction is exothermic or endothermic. Record this in your results table.

Sodium hydroxide and hydrochloric acid

1 Place the polystyrene cup inside the beaker.

2 Using the measuring cylinder, measure out 10 cm^3 of the sodium hydroxide solution.

3 Add the sodium hydroxide solution to the polystyrene cup.

4 Measure the temperature of the sodium hydroxide solution using the thermometer and record this into your results table.

5 Measure 10 cm^3 of hydrochloric acid using a measuring cylinder.

6 Add the hydrochloric acid to the polystyrene cup.

7 Work out the temperature change and, hence, whether the reaction is exothermic or endothermic. Record this in your results table.

Copper sulfate and magnesium

1 Place the polystyrene cup inside the beaker.

2 Using the measuring cylinder, measure out 10 cm³ of the copper sulfate solution.

3 Add the copper sulfate solution to the polystyrene cup.

4 Measure the temperature of the copper sulfate solution using the thermometer and record this into your results table.

5 Add 1 spatula full of powdered magnesium to the polystyrene cup. Stir with the thermometer and record the temperature after mixing into your results table.

6 Work out the temperature change and, hence, whether the reaction is exothermic or endothermic. Record this in your results table.

Sulfuric acid and magnesium ribbon

1 Place the polystyrene cup inside the beaker.

2 Using the measuring cylinder, measure out 10 cm³ of the sulfuric acid.

3 Add the sulfuric acid to the polystyrene cup.

4 Measure the temperature of the sulfuric acid using the thermometer and record this into your results table.

5 Add 1 strip of magnesium ribbon to the polystyrene cup. Stir with the thermometer until the magnesium has dissolved and record the temperature after mixing into your results table.

6 Work out the temperature change and, hence, whether the reaction is exothermic or endothermic. Record this in your results table.

Learning from practicals in action

At the end of this experiment, review the results with the students. Draw out key learning from their results tables, reinforcing that exothermic reactions give out heat and endothermic reactions take in heat.

If students have any findings that don't support this key learning, explore why this is so. Unexpected results in most secondary school practicals are likely to be the consequence of an error in procedure or materials, so explore this as part of the student journey towards thinking like scientists. Students can develop their disciplinary knowledge by understanding that experiments can have errors and that these errors can be compounded by poor experimental procedure. A strong way to explore this is to ask students to identify possible errors in an experiment and say how they could be minimised by changing the procedure.

Burning food to measure its energy content

In this practical you will ask students to burn various common foods in order to measure their energy content.

Equipment and reagents

- Thermometer (–10 to 110°C)
- Boiling tube
- Measuring cylinder, 25 cm^3
- Bunsen burner
- Heat-resistant mat
- Mounted needle
- Stand and clamp
- Balance, weighing to 0.1 g
- Various foods to be tested (for example, crisps, marshmallows, corn snacks, popped corn, bread, potatoes)

Setting up the practical

Consider how students are going to access the resources needed. It might be that each group of students can be given individual containers of each food to be tested, or they might need to go and collect these things from a central supply. If the latter, consider how you can avoid congestion around the equipment; perhaps each group nominates one member to collect equipment, or just have a few groups collect equipment at one time.

Give students a copy of the method (page 120) and allow them time to read it through. To support students with the literacy demands of the method, you could read the method aloud, asking questions to check understanding as you go.

Give students a copy of the results table or ask them to copy the one on the next page.

Food	Mass of food / g	Temp of water before heating / °C	Temp of water after heating / °C	Temp change / °C	Energy absorbed by the water / J	Energy absorbed per gram of food / J/g

Teacher in action

Display a food label showing the energy content of the food and use this to begin your discussion. Ask questions like this:

■ How do scientists find out how much energy a food contains?

Answer: by burning food and measuring the temperature change.

Be sure to stress that, although students are handling food, this is a science laboratory and eating the food would be dangerous and is not allowed at any point during the practical.

Next, demonstrate the method using one of the food samples provided. Measure out the required water using a measuring cylinder and then clamp the boiling tube at an angle. Weigh out the food sample, before mounting it on the needle.

To develop disciplinary knowledge, as you go, assess the students' understanding of the practical method by asking them to prompt you about next steps:

■ Now I've set up the boiling tube, what shall I do next?

Answer: add the water to the boiling tube.

■ How much water should I add?

Answer: 10 cm³

■ How am I going to measure out the water?

Answer: using a measuring cylinder.

To demonstrate the burning of the food, first light the Bunsen burner. This may be a time to review good Bunsen burner practice:

■ How should the Bunsen burner be set up before we light it?

Answer: with the collar closed.

■ What colour flame should the Bunsen burner have when not in use?

Answer: the yellow safety flame.

With the Bunsen burner on a blue flame, demonstrate lighting your chosen piece of food and use it to heat the boiling tube of water. Finally, take a temperature reading. Remind the students that they are trying to figure out the energy given out by each piece of food.

Guide the students in safely collecting the equipment needed, bearing in mind the layout of the room and the way in which your technicians have provided the equipment. While students carry out the practical, you should support the groups in carrying out the work and keep them on task. Stand in a position where the entire class is easily visible, so you can spot those students who might need some focused support during the practical. Concentrate your support on ensuring students are following the instructions with scientific precision and in a safe manner.

Students in action
Students should follow the instructions below to carry out the practical.

1 Measure 10 cm^3 of water into the boiling tube.

2 Clamp the tube in the retort stand at an angle (as your teacher did), over a heat-resistant mat.

3 Weigh a small piece of food and record its mass.

4 Measure the temperature of the water and record it in your results table.

5 Fix the food on the end of the mounted needle.

6 Light the food using a Bunsen burner (use the blue flame, before returning it to the yellow safety flame), and immediately hold it about 1 cm below the boiling tube and above a heat-resistant mat.

7 Once the food stops burning, stir the water with the thermometer and record the temperature.

8 Empty the boiling tube and refill it with another 10 cm^3 of cold water.

9 Repeat the experiment using a different food.

Learning from practicals in action

Once the practical is completed and students have tidied away their equipment, use some sample results to demonstrate how to calculate the total energy given out and the energy given out per gram of food. Then ask students to calculate the total energy given out and energy per gram for their own food samples.

This experiment also lends itself to a discussion of causes of inaccurate results in science experiments. In this experiment, not all the energy released from the food will be used to heat the water. Efficiency could be improved by using a draught screen or a bomb calorimeter.

Students should come away from this experiment with an understanding of:

- how to measure the energy content of a food
- how to calculate energy given out during an exothermic reaction
- factors that cause inaccurate results in this kind of experiment
- how these factors could be addressed.

Teaching electric current and voltage in physics

Electricity is a fundamental topic in the study of physics. However, core concepts such as how electricity flows around a circuit, the differences between *voltage*, *current*, *charge* and *potential difference*, and how these relate to each other, are often misunderstood by students. In this section, we will explore effective teaching approaches for this important area of physics teaching.

Direct explanation and examples

Before students learn about current and voltage, they should have a prior understanding of the ideas of electrostatics. They need to understand that particles can be charged, either negatively or positively, and that electrons are negative particles. With this knowledge, students should be ready to learn about current and voltage.

Define how electricity moves through circuits and what is carrying this electricity. Tell students that electricity is the movement of electrons, that they are negatively charged and that they move from the negative side of a power supply or battery, through the wires and components of a circuit, towards the positive side.

This is a good moment to look at why certain materials conduct and others don't. Tell students that 'conductors' are objects through which electrons can move easily, and specifically that *metals* are good conductors. This movement of negatively charged particles (electrons) through the circuit is electricity. Back up this description with a diagram or simple animation to reinforce the idea you are sharing. Next, we need to define 'current' for our students. We should be telling students that we can measure the amount of electricity flowing through a circuit by using the current. We formally define current as 'the rate of flow of charge'. Point out that the charge that is flowing comes from the movement of charged particles (the electrons).

With this definition in mind, you should provide students with the equation for current:

$$\text{current} = \text{charge/time}$$

$$I = Q/t$$

When looking at this equation, be sure to point out the units for each part: current, I, in amperes (A), charge, Q, in coulombs (C) and time, t, in seconds (s). Demonstrate how the equation can be arranged with *charge* or *time* as the subject, giving rise to the more memorable form of the equation $Q = It$. Model doing some calculations, working out the current when given the time and the charge, or the charge when given the time and the current. Be sure to emphasise the correct use of units when modelling your answers.

After modelling how to do these calculations, let the students do some guided practice, working through sets of similar calculations, rearranging the formula and giving correct answers with correct units.

Once you have taught students about current, progress to teaching voltage and resistance. When teaching these, follow a similar sequence to the one you used to teach current:

- Introduce the idea.
- Define it.
- Examine the relevant equation.
- Model how to use the equation.
- Guide students to practise doing calculations.

Using visuals

Visuals can be highly effective in helping students come to terms with the ideas of current, voltage and resistance. Pictures and animations can allow students to 'see' electrons flowing round a circuit, and current can easily be understood as the number of electrons moving round the circuit per second.

While using electrons in your diagrams and animations is good, it can help to relate the movement of electrons around the circuit to analogous ideas that students can experience in the world around them. This might mean replacing the electrons and the wire they travel in with cars on a road. This is a simple and effective way of grasping the concept of current (how many cars travel down the road per minute) and resistance (how wide the road is), with components such as resistors being represented as areas of the road that are narrower.

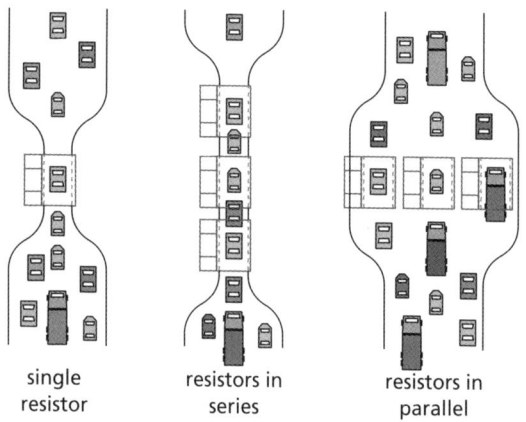

single
resistor

resistors in
series

resistors in
parallel

▲ Figure 16 Using an analogy of cars on a road can help students to
understand the concept of current and resistance

Another easily understood visual represents the flow of electricity around a circuit as the movement of water through a set of pipes. In this model, the volume of water moving around the circuit per unit time represents the current, and the resistance at points in the circuit is represented by the width of the pipes (narrower pipes having a higher resistance). In this model, voltage can also be represented. A battery or power supply can be thought of as a pump that pushes the electrons around the circuit. In the water model, the voltage applied by a battery or power supply can be equated with the force by which a pump pushes the water through the pipes.

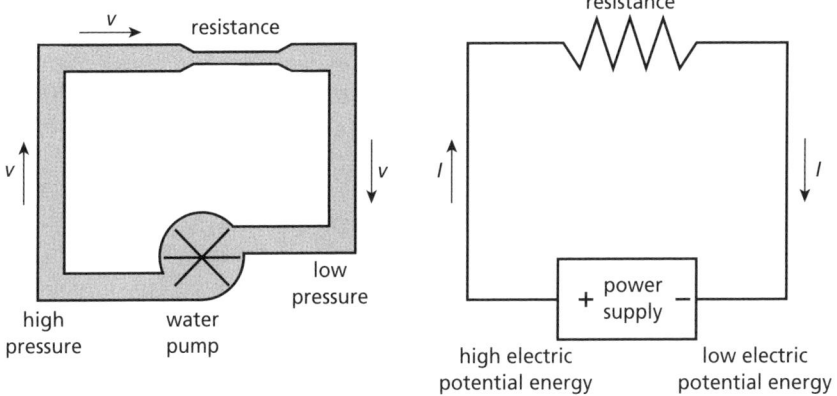

▲ Figure 17 A comparison between the flow of water and electricity

Virtual simulations, such as those created by the PhET Interactive Simulations project at the University of Colorado Boulder (https://phet. colorado.edu/en/), can also be highly effective in showing students how electrons move around a circuit, and the effects of changing voltage and resistance on the movement of these electrons. Interactivity allows students to see in real time how the changes they make to a circuit affect the electrons and the outputs, for instance how brightly bulbs in the circuit would shine.

Practicals as experiential learning

The key experiential opportunity when looking at the ideas of current, resistance and voltage is building circuits. Students can alter the circuits, by changing components, adding resistors and moving the order of components, and observe how this impacts the behaviour of the components in the circuit.

Building a simple circuit

A simple but effective practical opportunity involves asking students to build a basic circuit containing a bulb/lamp, a power supply and a resistor. Students can vary the voltage from the power supply (or, if using batteries/cells, they can add more cells to the circuit) and observe what happens to the brightness of the bulb. They can then repeat the process, this time keeping the voltage fixed and altering the resistance (either by changing the resistor in the circuit or by using a variable resistor), and again observe what happens to the brightness of the bulb.

Once observations of the brightness of the bulb have been made, students can use a voltmeter and ammeter to measure the voltage and current in their circuits when they make the same changes. Next, challenge them to explain the brightness of the bulb in their circuit using the readings from the voltmeter and the ammeter.

Measuring the resistance of a length of wire

A common experiment sees students measuring how the resistance of a piece of wire changes with the length of the wire. This allows students to gain hands-on experience of measuring current and voltage and using these measurements to calculate resistance.

Equipment and reagents
- Piece of constantan wire (sometimes called Eureka wire) about 100 cm in length
- Low-voltage power supply
- Variable resistor (rheostat)
- Switch
- Connecting leads
- Crocodile clips
- Tape
- Heat-resistant mats
- Ruler

Setting up the practical
The constantan wire should be mounted onto the heat-proof mat using the tape, so that crocodile clips can be attached at various points, and the length between these points should be measured using a ruler. It may be possible for the technicians to do this beforehand, to save time in class. Many technicians have a setup for this practical already made.

Consider how students are going to access the resources needed. It might be that each group of students can be given individual containers of equipment, or they might need to go and collect these things from a central supply. If the latter, consider how you can avoid congestion around the equipment; each group could nominate one member to collect equipment, or just have a few groups collect equipment at one time.

Give students a copy of the method (page 127) and allow them to create a results table of their own or copy the one below.

Length of wire / cm	Current in the wire / A	Voltage across the wire / V	Resistance of the wire / ohms (Ω)

Explain to the students that they are going to investigate how changing the length of a piece of wire affects its resistance. A recap of some key terms here would be beneficial:

- What do we mean by resistance?
- What is current?
- What is voltage?

Show the students how to set up the circuit. The use of a circuit diagram on the board or a virtual simulation of the circuit (such as those from PhET interactive simulations) may help students to visualise how to put the circuit together. While demonstrating how to build the circuit, you can ask students to guide you, developing their disciplinary knowledge:

- Where should we place the ammeter?

  Answer: in series with the wire.

- Where should we place the voltmeter in the circuit?

  Answer: across the wire being tested.

Once the circuit is constructed, use questions to the students to guide you as you take the first reading:

- How far apart on the wire should the crocodile clips be placed?

  Answer: 10 cm

- What voltage should the power supply be set to?

  Answer: 1 V

- What should I do if the current on the ammeter reads greater than 1 A?

  Answer: use the variable resistor to change the current to less than 1 A.

While demonstrating the practical, be sure to indicate the main safety points. The voltage should be kept to 1 V, and the circuit should only be kept on for the minimum amount of time to take the readings. This is to ensure that the wire does not become too hot.

While students carry out the practical, the teacher should support the groups in carrying out the work and keep them on task. Stand in a position where the entire class is easily visible so you can spot those students who might need some focused support during the practical. Concentrate your support on ensuring students are following the instructions with scientific precision and in a safe manner.

Students in action

Students should follow the method below to collect readings for the current and voltage for different lengths of wire:

1 Set up the circuit as demonstrated by your teacher.

2 Attach the crocodile clips to the wire 10 cm apart.

3 Set the power supply to 1 V.

4 Turn the switch on.

5 If the ammeter reads above 1 A, use the variable resistor to change the current until less than 1 A is available.

6 Record the voltage from the voltmeter and the current from the ammeter into your results table.

7 Turn off the switch.

8 Repeat steps 1 to 7 but increase the distance between the crocodile clips by 10 cm each time until you have eight different readings.

9 Calculate the resistance in the wire for each of your lengths, using the formula R = V/I, and add it to your results table.

10 Plot a graph of length of wire (x-axis) versus resistance (y-axis).

Learning from practicals in action

When students have plotted their graphs, ask them to describe the results they have obtained.

- Are the results proportional or not? How do they know?
- Are the results directly proportional or not? How do they know?

Students should come away with an understanding of:

- the relationship between the length of a wire and its resistance
- how to build a circuit to measure both voltage and current
- how to calculate the resistance when given voltage and current.

Teaching forces in physics

Forces is another fundamental topic in physics that recurs on the curriculum throughout secondary school and into further study. Here, we will examine approaches to some introductory concepts in forces.

Direct explanation and examples

When teaching forces, start with the very simple question 'what is a force?'. At its most basic, we can define a force as a *push* or a *pull* that changes a substance's motion or its shape. This definition should be accompanied by examples: pushing a block along a surface, pulling on a door to open it, the wind pushing a sail on a boat, or two teams pulling on the ends of a rope in a tug of war.

Once we have established the idea of a force, we need to introduce the idea that forces act in *pairs*, so that for any force there is an equal and opposite reaction. Demonstrate this to your students. Push on a wall and ask them some questions. 'Does the wall move when I push on it? Does the wall change shape when I push on it? Why don't I fall through the wall when I push on it?' Lead them to the answer that you don't fall through the wall because as you push on the wall, there is a force pushing you back from the wall in opposition to the push you are putting on the wall. There are pairs of forces acting in this scenario.

Give students further examples: drop a book onto a desk and explain the reason that the book fell initially was the force of gravity pulling it down. Why didn't it fall through the desk? The desk must be pushing it up, acting against gravity. You can give other examples, for instance a ball bouncing off a wall. For its direction to change when it hits the wall, the ball must have a force acting on it. This force comes from the wall when the ball hits it.

Now our students are equipped with a basic concept of a force and know that they act in pairs, they can learn about some more complicated types of forces that occur. A good next step might be to teach non-contact forces. These key forces are *gravity*, *magnetism* and *electrostatic forces*.

- Start with gravity. Demonstrate dropping something. Why did it change direction and fall downwards? It was pulled downward by a force called gravity. This force doesn't have to touch the object to push or pull it; it can act at a distance. It is a non-contact force.

- Attracting some small metal objects to a magnet can be used to show another non-contact force, magnetism. Show that the magnet can only attract objects that are close to it. Ask the class why this might be. (It's because non-contact forces get weaker the further away you are from them.)

- Demonstrate electrostatic non-contact force by using a statically charged plastic rod to bend the flow of some water running from a tap.

The next concept to introduce is the idea of directionality: that forces push or pull an object in a certain direction. Take a picture of a car driving down a road and label the forces that act on the car and their direction.

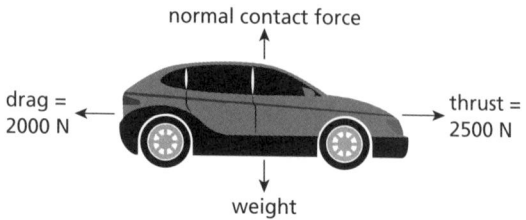

normal contact force

drag = 2000 N

thrust = 2500 N

weight

▲ Figure 18 The forces acting on a car in motion

In Figure 18, we can see that the thrust is pushing the car forward and is opposed by the drag or the air resistance. The car is being pulled down by its weight due to gravity but is being pushed back up by the reaction from the ground.

Finally, we can introduce the ideas of the size of the force, and balanced and unbalanced forces. Explain that some forces are bigger (stronger) than others and that we measure forces in a unit called Newtons. Take the example of a tug of war. If two teams pull on the rope with the same force (say 1000 N each), what happens to the rope? Nothing. The two teams cancel each other out and the rope stays put. But what if the team pulling to the left increases its effort and starts to pull at 1100 N? Now, there is an overall resultant force of 100 N pulling the rope to the left. The rope will change direction and move to the left. Go through other examples using the tug of war but changing the numbers.

Extend your discussion to the car. If the car is travelling at 30 mph and the drag and thrust are constant, what happens? It keeps moving at 30 mph. What if the thrust increases? The car will accelerate and move faster. If the brakes are applied, increasing the forces acting against the thrust, it will decelerate.

Newton's first law is a big source of misconceptions for students. Students often think that stationary objects have no forces acting on them and that objects moving in one direction at a constant speed have a resultant force in the direction they are moving. Be very clear that a resultant force means that an object *accelerates* in that direction. If all the forces acting on a moving object are balanced, the object keeps moving at the same speed as it did before (and a stationary object with balanced forces stays stationary).

This is just the start of exploring forces. Moving forward with students who understand the above concepts, the next step would be to look at the formula $F = ma$ and do some calculations, but just getting as far as an understanding of balanced and unbalanced forces represents a success in this large and complicated section of learning for students.

Using visuals

Visuals can be extremely useful in teaching forces. While students can't see the forces acting on objects, they can look at familiar objects doing familiar things and start to think about the forces that are acting on them. What effect do these forces have on these objects, and how do they explain their motion and behaviour?

Introduce students to pictures of everyday objects and ask them to add arrows showing the direction and name of the forces acting on them. Initially, these diagrams can be very mundane – a book resting on a table, a car driving along a road, or a plane in flight – and eventually more obscure, such as a skydiver before and after opening their parachute, or a rocket taking off.

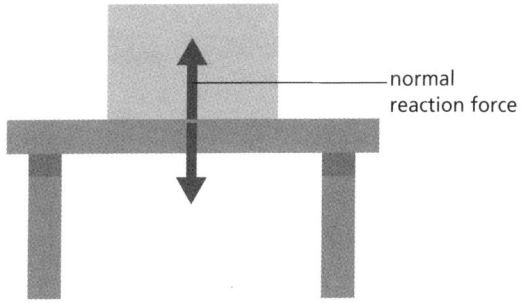

normal
reaction force

▲ **Figure 19 The forces acting on a box on a table**

With the visual of a box on a table in Figure 19, there are only two forces to label. Students should identify the force acting down, and explain why the object on the table doesn't move.

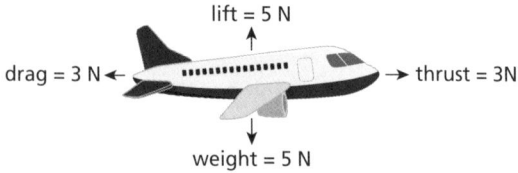

▲ Figure 20 The forces acting on an airplane

With the example of a plane in flight in Figure 20, naming the forces correctly and making sure they are labelled in the correct direction is important.

We can also ask students 'what happens if … ?'. What happens if the thrust is increased? What happens if the lift is less than the force of gravity? What happens if the plane is flying and the up and down forces are balanced and the left and right forces are balanced?

The idea of resultant forces can also be reinforced by diagrams. Give students a picture showing a tug of war and the forces being exerted by the two teams. Ask students to work out the resultant force and draw an arrow on the diagram with a value for the force. Figure 21 would be a good example of the type of visual to use.

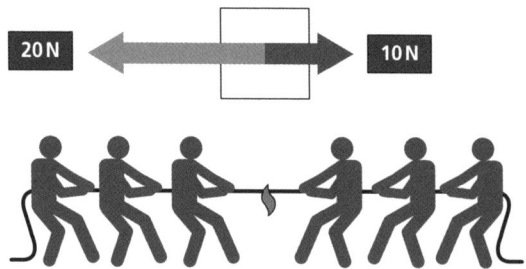

▲ Figure 21 The forces at play in a tug of war

There are also simulations that let you demonstrate these same examples to your students. The excellent PhET simulations allow you to vary the strength of the two teams in a tug of war, calculating the resultant force and showing which way the rope will move. This can be found at: https://phet.colorado.edu/en/simulations/forces-and-motion-basics

Diagrams showing resultant force are not limited to tugs of war but can be extended to any object. For example, Figure 22 is a similar diagram showing a car. Hinge questions can help the teacher to assess the level of student understanding and the presence of common misconceptions.

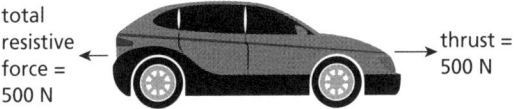

total resistive force = 500 N ← → thrust = 500 N

▲ Figure 22 The resultant force of a moving car

The car in Figure 22 is travelling at 25 mph with a thrust of 500 N and a total resistive force of 500 N. What happens to the speed of the car over the next 30 seconds if the forces acting on it remain unchanged? Answer options include:

1 The car will speed up.

2 The car will slow down.

3 The car will keep travelling at the same speed.

4 The car will stop.

Students who choose answer 3 have likely grasped the idea that no resultant force on an object means its speed remains constant. Students who choose answer 2 or 4 have the misconception that when forces are balanced, the object is stationary. A stationary object does have balanced forces, but not all objects with balanced forces are stationary. Students who choose answer 1 have not understood the role of resistive force.

Practicals as experiential learning

Practical work in this area allows students to connect the abstract concepts they have learned about forces to everyday objects and familiar experiences.

Drag force due to friction

Students can measure the force needed to pull a block of material (normally a wooden block) along different surfaces to find out how the degree of force that opposes the motion (i.e. friction) varies with different surfaces.

Each student will need access to a standard block that can be attached to a newton meter and pulled horizontally across the surfaces. Each student starts by placing their block onto their bench and pulling the block slowly along it, recording the force needed to *just* move the block. Students then repeat this process by placing their block of wood onto different surfaces

– sandpaper, rubber matting, a layer of cling film, a layer of cling film with a small amount of vegetable oil on it – and record the force needed to just move the block in each case.

Once students have their results, initiate a discussion of how the surface affects the force needed to move the block. Why does the rough surface take more force? The answer is that the force resisting the motion is greater, and so to unbalance the forces and move the block, you need to apply more force.

Weighing things: calculating mass on different planets

In this experiment, students look at the difference between the *mass* of an object and its *weight*. That is, the difference between how much of an object there is (its mass) and the force that pulls it towards the Earth (or whichever planet it happens to be on) – its weight. Ask students to move around the room to a number of different weighing stations, each of which represents a different planet in our Solar System. At each station, students will be asked to measure the weight of a container that has a supposed mass of one kilogram using a newton meter. Of course, the objects at each station don't physically have a mass of one kilogram, rather their mass has been tailored to give the correct results for the planet they are supposed to be on.

You will need to set up the stations shown in the table:

Planet/station	Actual mass (kg) of container representing a 1 kg mass on that planet
Earth	1
Mercury	0.5
Mars	0.38
Jupiter	2.8
Saturn	1.1

Each container should stay at its own station and ideally should be sealed and opaque, so that students can't see the masses inside it. Once they have measured the weights of the containers on the different 'planets', they can calculate the gravitational field strength of each planet. A discussion can follow about the difference between the mass and weight, and why the weight is higher on some planets and lower on others.

Running with parachutes

In this experiment, students will find out how hard it is to run while wearing a small parachute. You will need a set of running resistance parachutes and some stopwatches. You may need to borrow the right kind of equipment from the PE department in your school.

Mark out a fixed distance, say 40 m, for the students to run across. Ask pairs of students to time how long it takes them to run the distance unencumbered, recording a time for both partners. Next, the students will repeat the run wearing the resistance parachute. They will find it much harder and it will take them much longer. Discuss why it was harder to run while wearing the parachute. Point out that the weight of the parachute will have made little difference. It is the resistance – the force opposing them running forward – that makes it harder and take longer.

Ultimately, the real reason for doing this is giving the students the chance to experience a different force acting on them. The fact they have to work harder and exert more force to run while wearing the parachute is a strong piece of experiential learning that you can tie to a force diagram, or the idea of resultant force, in other lessons.

CHAPTER 8
WHAT STORIES PROVIDE POWERFUL HINTERLAND IN SCIENCE?

Telling the stories behind various scientific discoveries and theories is important to engage students and build their scientific literacy.

Scientific stories

Scientific stories not only engage students with the work of scientists and the excitement of discovery but connect the sometimes abstract business of scientific theory and method to real-world contexts and ethical, social and historical themes.

Biology

This selection of stories can provide powerful hinterland in biology.

Ignaz Semmelweis and handwashing

The work of Ignaz Semmelweis is good to share as an example of the history of medicine and the scientific method in practice. It also has a relevance to recent events, seen in the handwashing focus of public health advice during the Covid-19 pandemic. Semmelweis noticed that in two maternity clinics, the patients seen by doctors who had recently conducted autopsies had a much higher mortality rate than patients seen only by midwives. There were no handwashing routines, or gloves, in 1818. Semmelweis hypothesised that the doctors were transferring 'death particles' from the dead bodies to the mothers in the labour wards. He instituted handwashing between autopsies and deliveries, and the mortality rate dropped dramatically. He was ignored in his own time, but today, with our modern understanding of germs, handwashing saves millions of lives a year.

Gregor Mendel's peas

Mendel was an Augustinian monk in the 1800s who used observations of peas in his monastic garden to establish a science of heredity, giving 'he-looks-just-like-his-grandad' anecdotal knowledge of inheritance a scientific basis for the first time. By collecting seeds, keeping detailed observations and carefully pollinating and cross-breeding his peas, he was able to establish a scientific understanding of heredity, including the way some traits were dominant (tall or yellow peas) or recessive (short or green peas). This is a good story to explore disciplinary knowledge, as well as the ideas of heredity and inheritance themselves.

Rosalind Franklin, unsung hero of DNA

Watson and Crick won a Nobel Prize for discovering the structure of DNA, but it is always worth sharing with students the role of Rosalind Franklin in the discovery. Franklin had worked extensively exploring DNA and a photograph she had taken, called 'Photograph 51', showed that a double-helix structure for DNA must exist. You could even challenge your students to find a 2020 50p which was minted in tribute to Franklin and includes an image of her DNA photograph. The photograph (and Franklin's data) was later credited by Crick and Watson as giving them a clue to the structure of DNA, but Franklin herself did not win the Nobel Prize. Perspectives on her role could be discussed, including historical sexism in the field of science, but also that research functions as a collaborative effort, that researchers work together and build on each other's work – thus building student understanding of disciplinary knowledge.

Darwin and the theory of evolution

Darwin's theory of evolution by natural selection set the scene for the work of geneticists of the future. An exploration of his process for developing this theory really helps students understand how theories in science are hypothesised, developed, tested, shared and evaluated. At 22 years old, Darwin embarked on a 5-year voyage on the wooden ship *HMS Beagle*, working as a naturalist. In that time, he collected 1750 pages of notes, a 770-page diary and 12 catalogues of over 5000 samples. The more he observed and reflected, the more he started to question the biological theories of the time. Asking questions – 'Why have certain species become extinct?', 'Why are there no terrestrial mammals on oceanic islands?', 'Why are there species that seem very similar on places closely separated by the sea?' – led Darwin to develop his theory. This process took a long time and *On the Origin of Species* was published 23 years after he returned.

Alexander Fleming and the discovery of penicillin

In excellent contrast to Darwin's lifelong investment in developing the theory of evolution by natural selection, Fleming described the discovery of penicillin as almost accidental, and this can be a nice contrast to explore: 'When I woke up just after dawn on September 28, 1928, I certainly didn't plan to revolutionise all medicine by discovering the world's first antibiotic, or bacteria killer. But I suppose that was exactly what I did.' Through apparently sloppy laboratory organisation, a petri dish with staphylococcal bacteria in it was left by an open window and contaminated by mould – which seemed to kill the bacteria. Fleming isolated the mould and discovered its effectiveness against bacteria. The mould was a species called Penicillium, from which the name of the first antibiotic, penicillin, derives.

Chemistry

This selection of stories can provide powerful hinterland in chemistry.

Fritz Haber and the Haber Process

Fritz Haber studied to be chemist under Professor Robert Bunsen (of Bunsen burner fame). But he would go on to have a much darker legacy himself, becoming known as the father of chemical warfare. Before World War I, Haber was famous for inventing a method of extracting nitrogen from the air, which was used in fertilisers (so that more crops could be grown). Fertiliser made using the Haber–Bosch process is still used today to grow the food that supports the equivalent of half the world's population, and Haber received a Nobel Prize for this work. However, in World War I, the German army came to Haber for help with a more menacing project and, as a result, he developed chlorine gas as a weapon. Haber pushed his development, despite resistance from his generals and his own wife arguing against his plans, and in contravention of the Hague Convention banning use of chemical weapons in battle. The first time chlorine gas was used, it was estimated that 5000 people died in the trenches, and many more victims of gas attacks followed. After the war, Haber, who was Jewish, had to flee Germany as the Nazis rose to power. He was shunned by other scientists for his work on chemical weapons. He died in England, regretting his work on chemical weapons, only a few years before some of his own relatives would be killed by Nazis with Zyklon B gas, that had been developed in Haber's laboratory.

Black history and 20th Century chemistry

James Andrew Harris grew up in Texas and got his degree in chemistry in 1953. He served in the United States Army and then tried to find work as a chemist. However, he struggled because many employers in the US at the time discriminated against black men and would not offer him a job in science. After years of persistence, he started work as a radiochemist and then moved to a national laboratory in the Nuclear Chemistry Division as the first black chemist to work on discovering new elements. He was recognised as an excellent chemist and his team relied on him to prepare targets for use in experiments in difficult chemical separations. His team discovered two new elements: rutherfordium and dubnium. He was so talented that he became the leader of the Heavy Isotopes Team, despite being the only team member without a PhD.

Clarice Evone Phelps is an American nuclear research chemist who has been recognised as the first African–American woman to be involved in the discovery of a chemical element. Having served in the US Navy on the aircraft carrier USS *Ronald Reagan*, operating the nuclear reactor and steam generator chemistry controls, she worked on the team that discovered tennessine (element 117) in 2016. Phelps is an excellent example to share with students of a contemporary working chemist, only completing her undergraduate degree in chemistry in 2003.

Kekulé's dream of benzene

August Kekulé was a 19th-Century organic chemist; his most famous work was on the structure of benzene. The structure of benzene was an interesting scientific problem as scientists wondered how such an apparently simple structure – just six carbon and six hydrogen atoms – could be so stable. Professor Kekulé claimed he was sleeping by the fire and had a dream about a snake eating its own tail; he realised benzene must be structured into a circle, just like the shape the snake made in his dream. His discovery of the structure of benzene helped develop huge chemical industries, as benzene is used in paint, drugs and plastic. Today, it is disputed how far August Kekulé's dream about benzene was the real source of his inspiration, or whether it was just a great story, but it's a historical fact that the scientist himself told others that the structure of benzene came to him in a dream.

Hennig Brand and the discovery of phosphorus

Hennig Brand was a German merchant in the 1600s. He was a believer in the old alchemical idea that the human body was a microcosm of the Universe and, therefore, that everything that could be found in the Universe could also be found in the human body. Consequently, he believed that it should be possible to extract gold from the human body and that, if he could do this, he would become incredibly wealthy. Thinking about the human body and where there might be gold, he identified a liquid that the human body produces that has a kind of gold colour: urine. He decided to collect up as much urine as he could and tried to extract gold from it. In the basement of his house, he collected all the urine he could (mostly his own) and experimented on it, boiling it to concentrate it. Eventually, he started to distil it. The result was not gold, but a white solid that, when it came into contact with the air, caught fire. In fact, he hadn't found gold but a new element, phosphorus.

Mendeleev and the Periodic Table

In the 19th Century, many scientists were looking for ways to organise the known elements, but no one had yet come up with a satisfactory system. Mendeleev approached the problem by writing each element on a card and, as if setting out cards for a game of solitaire, attempted to organise them by atomic weight (the horizontal rows) and the properties of the elements (the vertical columns). The problem – although contemporary scientists didn't realise it – was that not all the elements had been discovered, and so the elements didn't seem to fit any pattern. Mendeleev's big breakthrough was to perceive that there were gaps due to elements yet to be discovered. He left spaces in his Periodic Table and predicted the characteristics of the elements that would fill them. For example, he predicted an element which he called 'Eka-aluminium'; this would be volatile, with a low melting point, an atomic mass of 68, soluble in both acids and alkalis, and with a density of 6.0. Later, an element was discovered and named gallium: it is volatile, with a low melting point, an atomic mass of 69.723, it is soluble in both acids and alkalis, and has a density of 5.91 – remarkably similar to Mendeleev's predictions.

Physics

The following historical stories can provide enriching hinterland context for students.

Newton and the discovery of gravity

The story that Newton was inspired to discover the theory of gravity by observing an apple fall from a tree in his garden is well known, but don't assume your students have heard it! It's a nice opportunity to explore a bit of myth-making; it is strongly disputed whether the story is in fact true in a literal sense (as the story did not appear in Newton's own lifetime and it frames him nationalistically as a quintessential English gentleman in his orchard). Nonetheless, the story–myth continues to resonate. Cuttings from the supposedly original tree at Woolsthorpe Manor, where Newton lived, have propagated trees all over the UK, including at Cambridge University, where Newton studied and wrote. A small chunk of the tree is in the Diamond Jubilee Coach used in the 2023 coronation, and cuttings and seeds have been sent into space.

The 'War of the Currents'

The commercial war between Tesla, Edison and Westinghouse in the 1880s and 1890s hinged on whether domestic power supply should be direct current (DC), as provided by Edison, or high-voltage AC supply, transmitted with transformers (of which Tesla was a pioneer and which Westinghouse brought to the US). The battle was a commercial one but played out in the media with some sensational moments. Prominent anti-AC campaigner Harold Brown staged several experiments in which he progressively shocked stray dogs (which had been collected by local children) with DC up to 1000 V. They survived, only to be shocked by 330 V of AC which killed them, supposedly 'proving' the dangerous power of AC. The first killing by electric chair was in 1890 but the lack of understanding of the current needed meant that the victim had to be shocked more than once to kill him: Westinghouse said that 'they would have been better using an axe'. Public outcry followed highly publicised cases in which workers on AC power lines were accidentally electrocuted to death. Eventually, the power companies merged, and the war ended with AC the victor.

Space pioneers of the Renaissance: Brahe, Copernicus and Galileo

Tycho Brahe was the last great astronomer before the invention of the telescope. He is known for the accuracy of his measurements with the naked eye and for improving instruments for observing the sky. He is perhaps even more famous for having a drunken duel in the dark with another student over which of them was the better mathematician. This resulted in much of his nose being cut off with a broadsword; for the rest of his life, he wore a prosthesis made of copper (or gold and silver for special occasions), held on by putty.

Copernicus was a Renaissance astronomer who formulated a heliocentric model of the Solar System (which put the Sun at its centre). His work built on that of medieval Islamic scholars which he had studied at university and challenged the model then currently accepted in Europe. Copernicus circulated his ideas in manuscript and by the early 1530s he had completed a longer work, *On the Revolutions of the Heavenly Spheres*. However, perhaps as he believed it would be controversial because of religious objections, it was only published shortly before his death in 1543. He dedicated his book to the Pope, but heliocentric theories proved lastingly contentious, so much so that 70 years after its publication, the book was placed on an index of forbidden books by the Catholic Church. Decades later still, the church would put Galileo in prison for heresy for publicly claiming the heliocentric model was the right one.

Katherine Johnson and the science of space flight

Katherine Johnson had a lot of firsts in her life: she was the first African–American person to go to graduate school in West Virginia, the first African–American NASA scientist and the first woman in her division to be credited on a report she had written. At university, she was so gifted in mathematics that new courses were created just to extend her study. Johnson worked as a 'computer' in the days before electronic computers; her role was to perform complex mathematical calculations for flights by 'computing' the results. She faced discrimination at work, as her workplace was segregated, with black workers forced to work, eat and use the toilets in separate rooms to white colleagues. The accuracy of her calculations on space flight trajectories (including for Apollo 11 and the return rescue flight for Apollo 13) was so impressive that astronaut John Glenn famously refused to go on a space flight before Johnson had checked the flight calculations.

Marie Curie: polonium, radium and radioactivity

Sometimes the hard work involved in stunning scientific breakthroughs can be obscured. In Marie Curie's case, hardship is absolutely fundamental to her story. Students should hear how she was initially denied higher education as women could not go to university in her home country of Poland. She worked, saved and taught herself for years, until she could afford to go to Paris to study. She achieved both maths and physics degrees, studying so hard she often forgot to eat and lived on just tea and toast for weeks at a time. She had barely enough money to live and resented any time away from her studies. She moved to a tiny room to be closer to the laboratory, and sometimes in winter was so cold in bed she would pile on all her clothes and even a chair to keep warm. When she was working on the discovery of radium, the research was so hard and exhausting for over four years that even her husband suggested giving up, but she loved science so much and was so determined that she kept on, eventually making her Nobel Prize-winning discovery. She won two Nobel Prizes in her lifetime (in both Physics and Chemistry), becoming the first person to achieve such a feat.

CHAPTER 9
HOW DO I MANAGE PRACTICALS?

What is the purpose of practical work?

The answer to this question very much depends on who you ask, but this helpful framework from Hodson (1990) covers the main purposes with clarity. They are to:

- enhance the learning of scientific knowledge
- teach lab skills
- develop certain scientific attitudes, like objectivity, open mindedness and willingness to suspend judgement
- grow insight into scientific method and expertise in using it
- motivate pupils by stimulating interest and enjoyment
- and we might add, to stimulate wonder and awe at the scientific world.

Unfortunately, much of the research literature is united in finding that these purposes are usually not well served by practical work: 'research is clear that practical work is not always effective. Often this is because its purpose has not been established, or because pupils are expected to do and think about too much at once' (Ofsted, 2021). Too often, practical work is used for the final two purposes – to engage pupils – but the scientific rigour of the first four principles is often lacking. Donnelly (1998) found that science teachers often do practical work because they believe that's just what science teachers do, rather than for a more learning-focused reason. With this attitude, the learning opportunities that practicals offer will inevitably be limited.

How can practical work help students learn substantive knowledge?

It is important to recognise that practical work is *not* best suited to helping students learn substantive knowledge. As practicals involve scientific method, it is tempting to see them as opportunities for students to 'discover' scientific knowledge. However, discovery-based learning has been widely discredited as a method for learning core knowledge.

Hodson (1990) suggests that practicals are to 'enhance' the learning of substantive knowledge, not as the core method of teaching it.

It is crucial that students be taught the relevant scientific knowledge *before* undertaking a practical. Carrying out the practical then becomes an activity that *rehearses* that new knowledge, helping to embed it in long-term memory. Substantive knowledge of the key science will be developed by seeing it 'in action', as long as the 'in action' moment comes *after* students have learned about the key principles through theory. For example, when teaching physics, it may seem reasonable to allow students to discover how current and voltage are related through doing a simple practical. However, as shown in the table below, this can lead to a disconnect between the scientific knowledge being taught and what happens in the outcome of the practical work. The practical work should be used to *reinforce* the theoretical knowledge that is taught, rather than as a way to discover it.

	Activity 1	Activity 2	Potential outcome
Effective approach	Theory-based teaching of the scientific principle first: current is proportional to voltage	Practical activity: build a simple circuit with a lightbulb, a fixed resistor and a power supply, and use an ammeter to measure current at different voltages	Students have a confident grasp of the content, reinforced by seeing it in practice. If the practical does not 'work', they are able to ask questions based on their prior learning, working like scientists to integrate practical results into an already established understanding of what they would have expected to see →

	Activity 1	**Activity 2**	**Potential outcome**
Ineffective approach	Practical activity first: build a simple circuit with a lightbulb, a fixed resistor and a power supply, and use an ammeter to measure current at different voltages	Theory-based teaching of the scientific principle: current is proportional to voltage	The link between the practical and theory is not clear to students. When they are carrying out the practical, they will be focused on the procedure not the science, as they did not have prior learning about the purpose and outcomes. If the practical does not 'work', the theory teaching will be complicated by students saying 'but I got a different result'

A simple format to structure the teaching of practicals is the 'predict – observe – explain' model. By taking students through these three steps in order, both substantive and disciplinary knowledge will be developed.

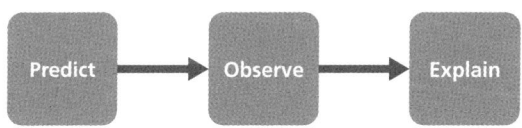

▲ Figure 23 The structure of a practical

How can practical work develop disciplinary knowledge?

Disciplinary knowledge is at the core of practical work. For each practical in the curriculum, it is helpful to set out exactly what disciplinary knowledge is being taught. If schemes of work and unit overviews are clear about this, it helps teachers to set success criteria and lesson objectives that develop disciplinary knowledge explicitly.

Disciplinary knowledge that might be covered in a practical includes how to:

- make predictions
- evaluate risks and work safely

- design an experiment
- use appropriate techniques and apparatus confidently
- record observations
- evaluate methods
- evaluate and present data
- propose questions for further study
- measure using the correct units
- analyse data using statistical approaches.

As with any learning, it is important to make these learning objectives clear, and then to share success criteria with the class. After the practical, make sure students have time to self-evaluate against these criteria (not just reflecting on the science learned). How well did they do at working scientifically?

Why is time spent mastering the use of apparatus so important?

Cognitive load theory tells us that working memory is limited. New information takes up more working memory than familiar information, and working memory is much more limited than we imagine.

In a practical, students are being asked to engage with two types of knowledge: the knowledge they need to carry out the procedure and the scientific ideas that underpin the practical. The demands of both can very easily overwhelm students' working memory. Expert scientists with vast experience in using scientific apparatus will be able to measure, weigh, mix and use the equipment using very little of their working memory; instead, they can use their working memory to focus on thinking about the science. But students will not have this level of fluency with the apparatus. They will use most, if not all, of their working memory to focus on correctly using the apparatus. They might even think that using the apparatus correctly means they have 'done' the practical well, before they have considered the science at all!

It is, therefore, an effective use of time in a science practical to build student experience and confidence with the apparatus. The more confident students become with scientific apparatus, the more likely it is that they will be able to focus on scientific learning.

How do you build a bridge between theory and practical lessons?

Reflect on each class you teach. Where would you situate them on the grid below?

A task is effective ...	... in the domain of observables	... in the domain of ideas
... at level 1 (what pupils do)	... if the students set up and operate the equipment so as to see what the teacher intended.	... if students think about the task using the ideas intended by the teacher.
... at level 2 (what pupils learn)	... if pupils are later able to show how to set up and operate similar equipment.	... the pupils are later able to show understanding of the ideas they were meant to use in carrying out the activity.

(Source: Abrahams, 2010)

In general, teachers are very good at putting the structures in place for moving their students from a notional 'level 0' to the point at which they can carry out a practical or think about a task by following carefully scaffolded prompts and instructions (level 1). However, moving students to level 2 can be more of a challenge. Just repeating a task with the same level of scaffolding is unlikely to enable students to move to level 2. This second level involves students learning to think metacognitively – that is, to think about their own learning in a reflective manner. To achieve level 2, scaffolding of a different sort is needed. Rather than focusing on *how* to complete the task, think about how you support students to think about their *own performance and understanding* of the task.

Some strategies that may help include the following:

- Using 'plan, monitor, evaluate'. For each task, be in the habit of explicitly telling pupils how to plan, monitor and evaluate their work. As you do so, remind students that you want them to *remember* the process, not just complete it. Use low-stakes testing for the process, not just the content, for example, by asking students to list three things they could do to plan a safe practical, or three things they could do to monitor if they are on track during a practical.

- Creating a checklist of questions for each stage of 'plan, monitor, evaluate', as shown in the table on the next page. Make the questions as specific to the topic and task as you can. Encourage pupils to refer to them often, until they carry out the three steps independently.

- Setting tasks that give students the chance to shine at level 2. For example, they could write a set of instructions for a Year 6 student explaining how to use this equipment or create a video which demonstrates their learning. Transformation tasks, asking students to repackage learning for a different audience or purpose, can be useful, especially as independent work, for showing the extent of their learning.

- Asking students to work in triads. Two students carry out the practical: the other student is a peer observer, focusing on how well the investigators are carrying out the instructions. Furnish the observer with a checklist of questions to fire at those doing the practical as they work: Why have you done it in that way? What are the risks at this point? How do you know it's safe right now? What will you do next and why? Are you happy with the way the work is going?

- Protect curriculum time for independent work at level 2. Plan time for students to work independently, and then allocate more time to reflect on their learning. The reflection is key, as this is where metacognitive learning takes place. Give students the chance to work independently, and then have them reflect on what they did well and what they will need to do differently in the future.

Plan	Monitor	Evaluate
• What resources do I need? • When I did a similar experiment, what worked well? • What did I learn from the demonstration? • What are the key points from the demonstration that I need to remember? • Having read all the instructions, what are the key steps? • How/where will I record my results?	• Am I doing well? • Am I checking the instructions carefully as I go? • Is there anything I need to stop and change or redo? • Are my results looking broadly as I expected? • Do I need to get any extra help (from the instructions, friend, board, teacher or textbook)?	• How did I do? • Did I use the equipment safely? • Did I work with accuracy? • Did I get the results I expected? • Did I work well with my partner? • Did I follow the instructions precisely? • Did I record my results effectively? • Is there anything I would do differently next time?

(Questions adapted from the EEF *Metacognition and Self-Regulation* (2018) guidance report.)

Scaffolding metacognitive reflection is crucial. Don't expect fully independent metacognitive reflection immediately. Plan to slowly withdraw teacher support over time.

Teacher demonstration or class practical?

A teacher demonstration has many benefits over a class practical:

- a reduction in the time needed for a whole-class practical
- fewer distractions from the learning
- an opportunity for the teacher to model the thought processes involved in using the equipment
- quick to set up
- allows the teacher to point out important points that might be missed in a whole-class practical
- enables the teacher to ask high-quality questions throughout the practical, engaging all pupils and developing learning in real time.

So, teacher demonstration is valuable, and should be used as an integral part of the curriculum. However, it is not a replacement for class practical work. It is still important for students to be able to practise practical work themselves, to build confidence with apparatus and to develop their own disciplinary knowledge.

How do I give effective instructions?

Effective teacher instructions are crucial in enabling students to carry out a practical. Instructions for practical work come in many forms, but the most used and often the clearest for pupils is a recipe-style set of instructions. This step-by-step set of written instructions lays out exactly what is to be done, including information like how much, how often, for how long, and so on. Instructions of this type help to lower the cognitive load on students. Rather than thinking about what is to be done at each step, students can instead focus on their observations and then their explanations of what is occurring.

Once you have given each student a recipe-style set of instructions, allow some time to read through the directions before instructing them to start the practical itself. Unfortunately, science teachers everywhere will know that this is not enough for the practical to be carried out effectively. Students often fail to follow the written instructions accurately!

But why? You've removed cognitive load and you've given time for students to look at the instructions. Studies show that students are often so eager to get on with the practical work that they skim over the instructions or skip parts, inevitably leading to mistakes.

A much more effective model is shown here:

1 Give students the instructions and allow appropriate reading time (say, 5 minutes).

2 Once students have finished reading, read the instructions aloud to the class.

3 If there are specific instructions that need elaboration, for instance how to use a certain piece of equipment, demonstrate while reading out the instruction.

4 Interrogate the class on the instructions: What do we do in step 1? What comes next? Why do we have to be extra careful in step 5? What kind of observation are we hoping to see in step 7?

5 Once you are happy that the students have understood, let them begin.

Many teachers will worry that going through these steps could use up a lot of class time, and time is often at a premium in a practical lesson. However, time spent ensuring that students understand what to do means that they will use their experimental time more effectively.

An extension of this way of giving instructions – which slows the process down even further but lets the teacher check that each instruction is completed before moving on – is the method of 'slow practical work':

1   The teacher reads the instruction aloud and demonstrates the step at the front of the classroom.

2   The teacher asks the students to complete the instruction using the demonstration as a model.

3   Once everyone has completed the instruction (this may take some prompting of certain students by the teacher), the teacher reads the next instruction and the cycle continues.

This slow practical variation further reduces cognitive load by allowing the teacher to actively demonstrate the use of equipment to the students and monitor class progress, helping students become proficient.

How do I work effectively with teaching assistants (TAs)?

There are a lot of elements involved in a practical, and the TA will hear the same instructions you give the class. In addition, they will need a solid understanding of the key skills you want the students to learn in the lesson, and how they can scaffold these for assigned students. A TA who is not an expert in science is likely to view success as 'the student completed the practical'. This is likely to lead the TA to support the student by helping them with each stage and encouraging a 'task completion' mindset. You might hear comments like: 'The next line says you need to put in 5 ml of the solution. Have you got your measuring cylinder? Okay, here is the solution to pour in.' Or even a simple, 'You've only got 10 minutes left, make sure you keep on task so you get finished.' Neither support is particularly helping the student develop as a scientist. Much better would be for the teacher to contact the TA (by email or quick informal chat) before the lesson to communicate the science focus for the practical and to give some prompts to help them work scientifically.

This is an example of the type of communication you might send:

Hi, We are doing a practical on extracting salt from rock salt in the lesson period 3 tomorrow. I've attached the instructions I will be giving the class. The key learning focus is going to be on the skills of separating and it would be great if you could ask them lots of questions about how and why they are doing the experiment, for example: 'How do you separate the salt? How can we separate the mixture? How do you know it has separated? What equipment do you need to separate it? What is happening now?'

How do I work effectively with technicians?

Science technicians hold a wealth of knowledge, skills and abilities, and a strong working relationship can help you to plan, organise and deliver practical work for your students. On the simplest level, your interaction with your technician as a teacher will be one of organisation. You will request them to prepare your equipment for practicals.

Ensuring that you give technicians ample time and clear instructions on what you want (for example, number of apparatus, volumes and concentrations of solutions) will help your practical run smoothly. Most school technicians will ask for practical work to be ordered to an agreed lead time and using an official order system; do everything you can to stick to these deadlines and systems.

Technicians, however, almost always offer far more than just a service preparing practical equipment for teachers. They tend to have a wealth of experience and so can offer advice on how practicals should be carried out, can give guidance on health and safety arrangements and how to set up unfamiliar pieces of equipment, and, in many cases, can act as an extra pair of hands in the classroom when doing complicated practical work. To get the best out of the teacher–technician relationship, include technicians in your planning and ask them for advice, especially if you are unfamiliar with the work to be done. By fostering a strong working relationship, you can ask your technicians to go above and beyond their normal routines, letting you practise unfamiliar practical work outside class time or even coming into class to demonstrate on your behalf.

How do I assess learning in and from practical work?

Because the key learning from a practical is not usually substantive knowledge, teachers don't need to follow a practical with an assessment of scientific ideas or knowledge. The substantive learning, which is being *enhanced* by the practical, should be assessed using all the normal tools of a teacher's trade (low-stakes testing, hinge questions, end-of-unit tests, marking work, questioning) as part of the wider scheme of work.

However, teachers *do* need to spend time assessing the disciplinary skills learned during a practical. Most learning from practicals will be in the disciplinary field. This is also a type of learning that lends itself less naturally to assessment, as discussed below; teachers need to be intentional and deliberate in assessing these skills.

Effective strategies to assess learning from practicals

The following three strategies are effective ways to assess learning and student understanding during practical work.

1 Hinge questions

Hinge questions are a good strategy for revealing the extent of student understanding, either as a plenary or starter. Consider the following example:

When a bar of chocolate melts, which statement best describes what is happening?

1   The chocolate surrounding the particles melts.

2   The particles move apart and keep moving apart.

3   Solid particles change to liquid particles.

4   The particles move about, keeping close together.

5   Hard particles change to runny particles.

The right answer here is 4. Answer 1 exposes the misconception that the chocolate and the particles are different things. Answer 2 is the hardest to explore, because in some ways the particles do move, but not in the way implied here (which would cause the chocolate to gradually expand in size). When a substance is melting, the particles move apart slightly, but then stay close to one another. If they kept moving apart, they would form a gas rather than a liquid. Answers 3 and 5 expose the misconception that there are solid or liquid particles – a state only arises from the interaction of many particles. Answer 5 foregrounds weak use of scientific vocabulary.

2 Self- or peer assessment with a success criteria checklist

Scientific skill	Done	Target for more practice
Can produce a clear results table, including correct units		
Can identify anomalous results		
Can plot a relevant graph, including labelled axes with units		

3 Low-stakes quiz

The following questions could be used after almost any practical:

1 What is a control variable?

2 Give an example of a control variable from today's experiment.

3 Why must we control some variables?

4 What is meant by the term 'anomalous result'?

5 What should you do if you have an anomalous result?

6 In today's experiment what may have caused an anomalous result?

7 Describe what your results show.

Challenges of practical work

How do I manage the classroom safely and effectively?

How you set out your classroom, and specifically how you set out the practical equipment within your classroom, can have a significant effect on how well a practical science lesson goes. In the worst-case scenario, poor placement of equipment and a lack of planning about how students will access the required apparatus could derail the entire endeavour. When the equipment has been placed poorly, such as all in the same place, a kind of scrum forms as students all try at once to access what they need. This, at best, wastes time and, at worst, is a safety concern. To avoid this, planning is necessary. The best solution is asking for the required equipment for each group to be placed into individual Gratnell trays (with each tray containing a full set of equipment). These trays can then be distributed to the students in their groups.

Sometimes this approach isn't possible: it puts a lot of pressure on the technician and occasionally the equipment may be too large to fit in one tray. When this happens, lay the equipment out at stations around the classroom so that there is no pinch point: place some equipment at the front, some at the back, some at the side. Then ask one student from each group to go to each station. This reduces the number of students at each collection point, allowing for calmer and simpler distribution of the equipment.

Each laboratory will be different, and you must plan an approach that works in the room you are using to minimise the issues of getting the equipment to the students.

How do I ensure students are learning, not just doing?

Through this chapter, it should be clear that just doing practical work does not help students to learn or become better at science. For the best learning experience in practicals, create a clear link between what students do, what they observe and how their observations can be explained using the ideas and knowledge they already have from previous lessons.

Further reading

Abrahams, I. (2010) *Practical Work in Secondary Science: A minds-on approach.* London: Continuum.

Donnelly, J.F. (1998) 'The place of the laboratory in secondary science teaching'. *International Journal of Science Education*, 20 (5), 585–96.

Education Endowment Foundation (2018) *Metacognition and Self-Regulated Learning.* Available at: https://educationendowmentfoundation.org.uk/education-evidence/guidance-reports/metacognition

Hodson, D. (1990) 'A critical look at practical work in school science'. *School Science Review*, 70 (256), 33–40.

Ofsted (2021) *Research Review Series: Science.* Available at: https://www.gov.uk/government/publications/research-review-series-science/research-review-series-science#curriculum-materials

CHAPTER 10

HOW DO I TEACH CROSS-DISCIPLINARY SKILLS IN SCIENCE?

Mathematics in science

A strong understanding of mathematical skills and how to apply them within a scientific context is key for science students, but achieving this is not easy. Transferring skills and knowledge from the mathematics classroom to the science classroom is a challenge. To help students achieve mathematical competence in science, it is important to build coherence between the science classroom and the mathematics classroom. Science teachers should work closely with the mathematics teachers in their school.

The first step is to gain an understanding of when the key mathematical skills needed in science are taught. Science teachers can then align their teaching to take advantage of this timing, by looking to build on concepts students already know from mathematics and placing them into a scientific context. Ideally, mathematical skills should be introduced in the maths classroom, rather than science teachers starting from scratch and overloading students by teaching them a new mathematical concept and then some new science that requires it. For instance, when teaching the Arrhenius equation during A-level chemistry, students benefit from prior knowledge of the laws of logarithms. This helps them to understand the rearrangement of the formula to make it useful for graphs. Planning to teach the equation *after* the mathematics department has introduced logarithms gives students a strong foundation to build on in their science lessons.

We also need to ensure that there is a coherence of language and method when it comes to using maths in our science lessons. If science and maths teachers teach line graphs using different terminology and methods, students will be confused and are likely to struggle in both approaches. It is vital that maths teachers and science teachers spend time conferring on shared language.

How can you ensure you have a coherent language and curriculum?

Communication is vital. Go and talk to the maths department. Ask them what language they use. Share your curriculum plans and identify when key maths skills are taught. Look for opportunities for shared CPD. Ask a representative from the maths department to come to science department CPD time, and present on how, when and why they teach the mathematical skills you want to see used in the science classroom.

Can we leave it all to the maths department then?

No! Even once we have ensured that our teaching is aligned perfectly with that of the maths department, science teachers can't wash their hands of the teaching of mathematical skills. Imagine a teacher introducing a task with this instruction: 'I know you learned how to draw a line graph in maths last week. Here's some data. Now draw me a line graph.' Blank silence would likely reign. Students have a hard time transferring skills from one subject area to another. Knowledge becomes compartmentalised into 'maths knowledge' and 'science knowledge'. As teachers, we must build bridges between these areas. It is important that we take the time to explicitly teach how to use the skills and knowledge acquired in maths lessons in the context of science lessons.

When asking our students to draw that line graph, take them step by step through the process, guiding them to help you construct the diagram using what they have learned in mathematics. Refer back to that knowledge, asking them, 'What did you do in maths? Can that help you now?'.

We also need to give students the opportunity to practise maths skills in a scientific context. Many resources exist that offer opportunities to practise maths skills in the context of science. The major learned societies, the Royal Society of Chemistry, the Institute of Physics and the Royal Society of Biology, offer many strong resources for students to practise their skills (for example, Maths skills for chemistry, a resource from RSC Educations available at: https://edu.rsc.org/resources/maths-skills-for-chemistry/4013899.article).

What about the differences between science and maths?

There are some areas where things are done differently in science and maths. Terminology is different, methods are different and expectations are different. When this arises, teachers should be up front and honest with students about it. Explicitly say, 'In science we do it like this'.

Going back to that line graph, in maths it might be called a scatter graph. Mathematicians draw best-fit lines differently to scientists; in maths, a best-fit line should always be a straight line, whereas scientists encourage students to look at the data and draw a curved best-fit line if needed.

A mathematician might spend a lot of time talking about correlation of the data from their graph; over in science, we are more interested in proportionality. These differences can be hard to teach and may be confusing for students, but – by knowing as much as you can about what is taught in maths – you can prepare yourself to focus on these key differences and make them explicit during your teaching.

Finally, remember that while an understanding of maths skills is crucial to science, this is not reciprocated. Mathematicians don't rely on the skills taught in science in the same way as scientists need those skills from maths. Be nice to the maths department, build that relationship and use their expertise to inform your teaching.

Reading like a scientist

For meaningful curriculum time to be given to teaching reading in science, it is important to realise that science teachers should not be being asked to teach generic reading skills. There is a set of reading skills that scientists use in order to authentically 'read like scientists'; when we talk about reading in the science classroom, we are talking about how to explicitly teach students *these* skills.

What reading skills do students need to know to be successful in science?

Reading in science is primarily an act of enquiry. Scientists read to be informed, to seek information and to find answers to questions. There are specific barriers students face when reading in science. Scientific texts are often full of complex subject-specific vocabulary. Texts are sometimes written in the passive voice, which can be unfamiliar to students. These challenges can slow down students, prove demotivating and, to those with certain SEND needs, are a real barrier to engaging with the subject.

What reading skills are helpful to teach science students?

Don't overcomplicate reading in science. Students will benefit from learning explicit strategies including:

- knowing what information they are looking for (prompt them always to read the question before they read the text)
- considering background knowledge – ask what they already know on the topic and what, therefore, they predict might be in the text
- skimming and scanning to find key information
- using the headlines and subheadings to help get an overall view of the content
- using glossaries proactively
- rereading with a purpose – taking a 'first glance' and 'second reading' approach
- asking questions to check comprehension at each stage of reading.

How can I teach reading skills within the science curriculum?

To teach each of the strategies outlined above, the simplest and most effective strategy is modelling. Pop a text up on a visualiser or PowerPoint slide and talk the students through your own process. Here is a script demonstrating teacher modelling of a reading task, with four key strategies highlighted.

> The first thing I'm going to do before we read this information on radioactivity is to read the questions and highlight the key words, so I know exactly what I'm looking for. Do you think I need to understand every word of this article to answer the questions? No – we are just looking for specific information, so that makes it a bit easier.
>
> Right, the second thing we are going to do is a quick prediction. What do we already know about these questions? [Quick class discussion]
>
> Now for the third strategy. Before we read, let's look at the headings and subheadings. Anyone got an idea from these signposts which paragraphs might have the answers we want? The heading of this paragraph looks like it might be useful.
>
> Fourthly, just remind me what to do if you get to a scientific word and you can't remember what it means. We've got the glossary here to help – and if the word isn't there, you can try to work it out from the context or even ignore it if the sentence isn't helping you with the question.

Another helpful strategy is to give students a reading checklist to use. You could even include this checklist as a display in the classroom.

Have you ...	Tick if you used this strategy
... highlighted key words in the questions?	
... brainstormed what you already know about the questions?	
... read the headline and subheadings first?	
... used the glossary to look up scientific words you don't know?	
... read the text twice – a 'first glance' and 'second reading'?	
... skimmed and scanned, looking for keywords to find the information you need?	
... noted any questions you have about the information?	

Current research suggests that there are benefits to teachers reading aloud to their students: modelling fluency and enjoyment of reading, and exposing students to more complex texts than they can read independently (Lemov, Driggs and Woolway, 2016). Be encouraged to read aloud to your students, whether from the textbook, texts for building cultural literacy or just scientific articles you enjoyed and want to share.

Writing like a scientist

This is a familiar situation to teachers everywhere: verbally, the student has answered every question accurately, but when it comes to writing answers, suddenly their work is brief or incorrect, just not on a par with the quality of their spoken explanation.

There are specific barriers to writing in science: the importance of using precise technical vocabulary, the need to write in an informative or explanatory mode and the challenges of structuring a response in an appropriate manner. It may also be that those confident verbal responses mask an incomplete understanding; it is often in written work that the teacher exposes gaps in learning. Struggling with the written side of science can be demotivating and stressful for students, making them think they are 'bad' at the subject.

For all these reasons, it is important that science teachers explicitly teach students how to 'write like a scientist'.

What writing skills do students need to know to be successful in science?

Writing is, in one sense, closely linked to reading. To answer exam questions, students must read the question, identify the command word and then write the correct style of response. The table offers guidance on different possible appropriate responses to common command words.

Command word	Written answer might include ...
State	... correct scientific terminology, for example respiration not breathing.
Describe	... sequence words to define steps in a process: first, then, next, finally.
	... observations. (Prompt students to say what they see.)
Compare	... comparatives: warmer, colder; faster, slower; more than, less than.
	... words to indicate similarities: similarly, further, in the same way.
	... words to indicate differences: however, in contrast, on the other hand.
Explain	... the word 'because', followed by a reason.
Evaluate	... similarities *and* differences. (Students need to know that 'evaluate' is similar to 'compare' and 'explain', but they need to include *both* sides of an argument.)
	... evidence for and against an opinion.
	... words to introduce a final judgement: in conclusion, overall, on balance.
Write	... a very short answer*.
	*Confusingly, only a 'short answer is required, not an explanation or a description' (see, AQA Education).

How can I teach writing skills within the science curriculum?

The following strategies can help students to overcome barriers to writing scientifically:

Focus on precision of written language

This is a habit that needs to be explicitly taught and drilled. A quick and effective strategy to make it clear to students how careful they need to be about choosing the correct word is to use a multiple choice question or a hinge question, for example:

Question: Which is the correct statement?

Possible answers:

1 In energy transfer, energy is *produced* from glucose.

2 In energy transfer, energy is *released* from glucose.

The correct answer is 2. Follow up with a quick discussion about why this is the correct answer.

Focus on vocabulary

Spelling of key scientific terms is important. Some words are associated with common mnemonic tricks to help remember their spellings. Otherwise, low-stakes spelling tests are proven to work.

Success criteria

As in any other teaching moment, success criteria or checklists can help students with written tasks. A brief success criterion might be 'Have you included a comparative word in your answer?'. An extended check list for evaluation is shown below:

Does your written answer include ...	Tick if completed
... signpost phrases for similarities – like 'similarly'?	
... signpost phrases for differences – for example 'on the other hand'?	
... comparatives – like 'better', 'warmer', 'faster', 'less than'?	
... a summary phrase – such as 'in conclusion' or 'overall'?	
... correct spellings of science vocabulary?	

Rehearsal and reflection

Giving students time for verbal rehearsal and post-task reflection will strengthen their written work. A simple cycle might be:

- 90 seconds to think in silence about their answer to the question
- 60 seconds to discuss their answer with a partner and say out loud what they will write
- 90 seconds to write their answer
- 60 seconds using success criteria to check their answer for accuracy and inclusion of key words.

Speaking like a scientist

Class discussion of scientific ideas can be an excellent way to help students organise information in their minds, letting them challenge each other's thinking, highlighting their preconceptions and misconceptions and allowing them to develop a critical way of thinking about data.

Mercer, Dawes, Wegerif and Sams (2004) assert that, for students to get the best out of discussions, clear rules for how to proceed should be in place. Their framework allows for all students to be involved and sets out clearly how the discussion should be conducted:

- All group members must contribute; no one member should say too much or too little. Team members should encourage those who are saying less.
- Every contribution should be treated with respect and listened to thoughtfully, and everyone should be allowed to finish.
- Each group must achieve consensus by the end of the activity, and the teacher may need to resolve differences.
- Every suggestion a member makes has to be justified – students should say what they think and why they think it.

Evidence from Bennett et al. (2010) has also shown that it is beneficial to give students stimuli presenting a range of views for debate. These could be as simple as a range of possible outcomes from a completed experiment. Ask students to debate which outcome is correct: Why is it correct? Who has the best explanation? Why is their explanation correct?

These stimuli allow students to form ideas of their own and can even be set up to challenge preconceived ideas. Students should not only select the best ideas and explanations, but try to think about *why* something is right or wrong – a key deeper-thinking skill.

How can cross-disciplinary links with other subjects support science teaching?

There are lots of moments in secondary education where productive cross-disciplinary links between subjects can support science teaching. Knowledge transfer between domains is cognitively difficult, and generally does not occur without specific effort. Having just completed an in-depth investigation into plate tectonics in geography, students may still come to a science lesson claiming to be unfamiliar with the words *core, plate, lava, magma, focus, Richter scale* and *epicentre* (even if they just aced their end-of-unit test on these very concepts).

But if we encourage students to bring their learning from other lessons to the science classroom, and vice versa, it will help them to develop mental connections between subject understandings in a mutually reinforcing way. They will build more detailed schema, with more connections between learning in their long-term memory, and their understanding of all subjects will be improved. Some connections that are worth exploring are shown in the table:

Subject	National Curriculum content	Science link
Geography	Physical geography relating to geological timescales and plate tectonics Rocks, weathering and soils Weather and climate, including the change in climate from the Ice Age to the present	Chemistry: • The structure and composition of the Earth • The rock cycle and the formation of igneous, sedimentary and metamorphic rocks
	Understand how human and physical processes interact to influence and change landscapes, environments and the climate; and how human activity relies on effective functioning of natural systems	Chemistry: • The Earth as a source of limited resources and the efficacy of recycling • The composition of the atmosphere • The production of carbon dioxide by human activity and the impact on climate →

Subject	National Curriculum content	Science link
DT	Understand and use the properties of materials and the performance of structural elements to achieve functioning solutions	Chemistry: • The order of metals and carbon in the reactivity series • The use of carbon in obtaining metals from metal oxides • Properties of ceramics, polymers and composites (qualitative)
DT (Food)	Understand and apply the principles of nutrition and health	Biology: • The content of a healthy human diet – carbohydrates, lipids (fats and oils), proteins, vitamins, minerals, dietary fibre and water, and why each is needed • Calculations of energy requirements in a healthy daily diet • The consequences of imbalances in the diet, including obesity, starvation and deficiency diseases
PE	Understand and apply the long-term health benefits of physical activity	Biology: • The impact of exercise, asthma and smoking on the human gas exchange system →

Subject	National Curriculum content	Science link
RSE	Key facts about puberty, the changing adolescent body and menstrual wellbeing The main changes which take place in males and females, and the implications for emotional and physical health	Biology: • Reproduction in humans (as an example of a mammal), including the structure and function of the male and female reproductive systems, menstrual cycle (without details of hormones), gametes, fertilisation, gestation and birth, to include the effect of maternal lifestyle on the fetus through the placenta
	Personal hygiene, germs including bacteria, viruses, how they are spread, treatment and prevention of infection, and antibiotics	Biology: • The relationship between health and disease • Communicable diseases, including sexually transmitted infections in humans (HIV/AIDS) • Non-communicable diseases • Bacteria, viruses and fungi as pathogens in animals and plants • Body defences against pathogens and the role of the immune system against disease
History	Challenges for Britain, Europe and the wider world 1901 to the present day	Biology • Communicable diseases including sexually transmitted infections in humans (HIV/AIDS) • The process of discovery and development of new medicines

How can you embed cross-disciplinary links into the curriculum?

At the most basic level, you can just drop cross-disciplinary moments into your lesson, for example, 'Today we are going to be looking at the properties of rocks. You have 90 seconds to discuss with a partner everything you learned about rocks in geography last term.'

If you have time, a more structured approach might be to work with other departments to identify shared content and map these onto your curriculum plans, to enable teachers to make links more effectively. There is no point asking students to brainstorm prior learning from personal, social, health and economic education (PSHE) on global warming if they aren't due to study it for another term. If you know that students have studied a topic in at least two timetabled subjects, a great activity is to get them to create a mindmap or poster showing their knowledge on the topic from *both* subjects, strengthening their learning by forcing them to make cross-disciplinary links. It's up to you if you let them use their books!

If you have even more time available, identifying key departments and engaging in co-planning is a great use of CPD time. Sit down with the DT department to share ideas for teaching the topic of materials. Co-plan with PE, focusing on how anatomy is taught. Find 30 minutes to work with the history department on how the history of medicine unit (for example) could interact with the biology curriculum.

Further reading

AQA Education. Available at: https://www.aqa.org.uk/resources/science/gcse/teach/command-words

Bennett, J., Hogarth, S., Lubben, F., Campbell, B. and Robinson, A. (2010) 'Talking Science: the research evidence on the use of small group discussions in science teaching'. *International Journal of Science Education*, 32 (1), 69–95.

Lemov, D., Driggs, C. and Woolway, E. (2016) *Reading Reconsidered: A practical guide to rigorous literacy instruction*. Hoboken, NJ: Jossey Bass.

Mercer, N., Dawes, L., Wegerif, R. and Sams, C. (2004) 'Reasoning as a scientist: Ways of helping children to use language to learn science'. *British Educational Research Journal*, 30 (3), 359–377.

STEM Learning, *Learning Skills for Science Skill 3 Scientific Reading*. Available at: https://www.stem.org.uk/resources/collection/3710/skill-3-scientific-reading?page=1

CHAPTER 11
HOW DO I ENGAGE MY STUDENTS BEYOND THE CURRICULUM?

How can I deliver the Gatsby benchmarks for careers in science?

The Gatsby Foundation sets out a number of benchmarks that indicate a school has good careers guidance (Chapter 2). The most important benchmark for science teachers to implement is the linking of curriculum learning to careers. The Gatsby Foundation suggests that:

> STEM subject teachers should highlight the relevance of STEM subjects for a wide range of career pathways ... [and that] ... by the age of 14, every pupil should have had the opportunity to learn how the different STEM subjects help people to gain entry to, and be more effective workers within, a wide range of careers.

Science teachers need to build opportunities into their lessons for students to see how their learning is directly applicable to careers. It is important that students gain an appreciation of entry requirements, the skills required and the day-to-day lives of workers in various jobs linked to the STEM subjects.

This sounds a lot, but it really is just about strong planning. When planning the science curriculum, opportunities to link careers to certain topics should be identified and then specific resources used to integrate these into the lessons. Some careers are easy to link to our science curriculum: for example, medical careers when studying the human body in biology; engineering when studying forces in physics; and forensic science when studying analytical techniques in chemistry. However, a little more thought is needed to properly integrate other careers into the curriculum. For instance, learning about a career as a welder links to the chemistry content about displacement reactions and the reactions of metals. Information about careers can be presented to students through simple slides such as that shown in Figure 24.

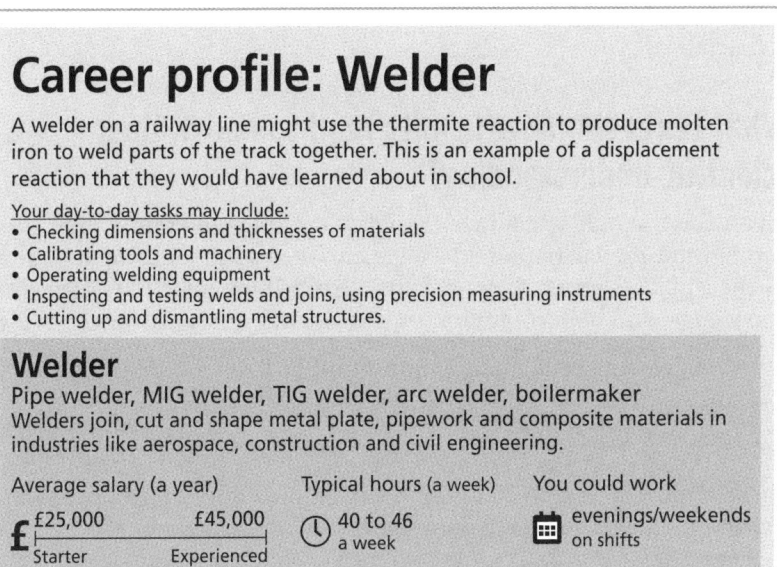

Career profile: Welder

A welder on a railway line might use the thermite reaction to produce molten iron to weld parts of the track together. This is an example of a displacement reaction that they would have learned about in school.

Your day-to-day tasks may include:
• Checking dimensions and thicknesses of materials
• Calibrating tools and machinery
• Operating welding equipment
• Inspecting and testing welds and joins, using precision measuring instruments
• Cutting up and dismantling metal structures.

Welder
Pipe welder, MIG welder, TIG welder, arc welder, boilermaker
Welders join, cut and shape metal plate, pipework and composite materials in industries like aerospace, construction and civil engineering.

Average salary (a year)   Typical hours (a week)   You could work

£25,000   £45,000   40 to 46   evenings/weekends
Starter   Experienced   a week   on shifts

Find out more: https://nationalcareers.service.gov.uk/job-profiles/welder

▲ Figure 24 Careers in science (Source: Science department, Dame Elizabeth Cadbury)

The Gatsby Foundation also advocates for schools to promote encounters beyond the curriculum, for example, through experiences with employers, employees and workplaces. Visits to science-based workplaces and talks from speakers about how science forms a part of their day-to-day role are extremely useful in informing students about possible careers.

Learning about careers and the world of work also has an important part to play in making science real for our students. Looking forward to the world of further study and work helps students to engage with the abstract nature of the subject by connecting it to the very concrete reality of their own future lives. It allows them to place the things they learn about in class into a concrete, real-world context, solidifying their learning.

What kind of careers should I promote?

When planning which careers to highlight, it is important to get a balance that is suitable for the students in your setting. Within many science classes across the country, there will be students with aspirations to go to university and pursue post-graduate careers. For others, non-graduate routes are more relevant. Getting the pitch right for your students is crucial.

What texts should students read to enrich their scientific understanding?

All teachers should encourage their students to read around their subject and beyond the curriculum. It helps enhance a student's understanding of the subject, gives them a better context in which to frame their knowledge, and helps maintain their academic curiosity for the subject.

When suggesting reading, it is important to focus on texts that explore four main areas: the history of science; science and its effects on the world around us; sources that answer students' questions; and those that widen the diversity of information presented to students about science. These types of reading matter complement what is going on in the classroom, making science seem more real and relevant.

We should avoid setting very academic texts, for instance, those looking at topics that are to be taught in coming years or higher key stages. For example, a student learning about equilibrium in KS4 chemistry is probably not best served by reading a text about how to calculate the equilibrium constant, as they will learn this if they take A-level chemistry. They would be much better off reading about the life story of Fritz Haber, his time serving in the German army as head of the chemical weapons division, his work on making ammonia to support Germany's agriculture and munitions industries, and his eventual flight from the Nazi regime. Here the student *may* learn some more about equilibrium in the Haber process, but will certainly gain an appreciation for the context, history and effect science has had on the world.

What can I do to promote science as a diverse and inclusive field of study?

Unfortunately, there are prevalent stereotypes and imbalances in science as a field of study and work. If we ask students to write an essay about a famous chemist who has made an impact in the field of study, it is highly likely they will choose a white European man: Mendeleev or Haber, for instance.

Many schools will have been involved in attempts to attract more girls into STEM. Science teachers have a crucial role in promoting diversity within the field, in deconstructing stereotypes and achieving social change by encouraging students to see beyond historical imbalances towards modern possibilities. There are some simple strategies science teachers can use to achieve these goals, which will be discussed in the next section.

Highlight the diverse history of science

Science today is a diverse field and science in history has been diverse. It is not enough to know this in the abstract, we need to make it explicit to students. Some simple ways to do this include:

- using displays in your classroom
- promoting books that explore diversity in science
- explicitly mentioning scientists from diverse backgrounds in your lessons
- choosing examples carefully, especially imagery of people working in science, to ensure positive messages are received that all are welcome in the field.

Explain the historical lack of diversity in science, rather than ignore it

It is a fact that many of the scientists on the curriculum are white European men. Teachers should not ignore or skirt around this.

It would be wilfully obtuse to teach the Periodic Table without mentioning Dmitri Mendeleev, John Dalton, Johannes Döbereiner and John Newlands. Instead, simply acknowledge the historical context of this fact, by saying something like this:

> *You might notice all the scientists involved in this development were white European men. This research was happening in the 1700s and 1800s, a very different time, when scientists were independently wealthy, or had rich patrons. It was a patriarchal time when women were largely denied access to scientific study, for example, by not being allowed to attend university. This helps explain why it was white men leading the research.*

By acknowledging the lack of diversity but also explaining it, you are helping students to recognise how society has changed and hopefully minimising any feelings of exclusion by providing historical context.

Proactively monitor practical work and scientific debates

In practical work and in discussions, there is potential for harmful stereotypes to be unintentionally perpetuated. In an Institute of Physics report (2017), researchers found that teachers unconsciously associate different words with girls and boys:

- words to describe boys – practical, hands on, lazy, vocal, confident
- words to describe girls – detailed, focused, hard-working, reserved, perfectionist.

Why do we use these words and what impact do they have? A teacher who unconsciously assumes boys will be 'practical and hands on' might be at risk of allowing boys to take the lead in practical work – thus giving them further opportunities to develop practical skills that students who are encouraged or allowed to sit back will not get. A teacher who unconsciously assumes girls are naturally 'reserved' might choose not to 'put them on the spot' with verbal questioning, a choice that accidentally minimises the learning opportunities offered to all students with equality. If we don't interrogate our biases, we are at risk of subliminally reinforcing expectations of behaviour that are socially driven, not learning driven.

The messaging, both implicit and explicit, must always be that all of science is for everyone. Science teachers should be alert to, and proactively challenge, stereotypes:

- Be conscious of your questioning technique and try to ensure all students are involved equally.
- In practical work, make it explicit that all students should be involved in every part of the experiment.
- Encourage students to identify and assume responsibility for roles in which they feel less confident (setting up the equipment or taking measurements, for example).

Seek out resources that promote diversity in science

The Gender Action in Science project has a toolkit of useful resources, including a series of posters for display in classrooms: https://www.genderaction.co.uk/gender-action-resources

The Royal Society has a collection of case studies about different aspects of diversity, from gender, to disability, to ethnicity: https://royalsociety.org/topics-policy/diversity-in-science/topic/

What is the role of trips in science teaching?

Taking students out of the classroom on trips is of tremendous value in science teaching. They are a major opportunity for inspiring students with the awe, wonder and excitement of science, and boosting engagement in the subject. Visiting museums, research centres, festivals and conferences, for example, can be particularly valuable for disadvantaged students. However, for all students, the opportunity to explore science 'in action' outside the school will increase their cultural capital.

When planning trips, think about how you can make them purposeful for learning. For example, if visiting the Science Museum in London, you could just let the students explore, but it could make the experience even richer if you give students some prompts and then follow up once back in the classroom. Prompts could be substantive (finding out scientific facts to bring back) or disciplinary (zooming in on information about working scientifically).

Museums and science organisations usually try to encourage school trips, so often have sections of their webpages for schools, specifically to provide resources and help teachers plan a great visit. Research the right experience for your students by thinking about the practicalities of visits and the value of different types of trips:

- What local opportunities are there, tying in with the local context and raising student engagement with science in the local area?
- What venues of national cultural importance might be relevant and interesting?
- Is there scope for international trips (perhaps to CERN or NASA)?

In biology, check out organisations such as the Field Studies Council, which helps schools organise residential fieldwork in locations all over the country.

What organisations offer opportunities beyond the curriculum?

There are many sources of resources for science teachers. Although sources such as the *Times Educational Supplement* (TES) have a wealth of resources, those provided by learned societies or subject-specialist associations have the advantage of expert input from a range of specialists, both researchers and educationalists.

- The Royal Society of Chemistry offers thousands of free teaching resources, competitions and CPD for teachers.
- The Royal Society of Biology offers free resources, competitions and outreach opportunities.
- The Institute of Physics offers free teaching resources, with a strong focus on supporting trainee teachers and retaining teachers in the profession.
- The Field Studies Council offers residential fieldwork trips for biology students at a number of different locations.
- The Salters' Institute is a registered charity promoting chemistry for all age groups, with a focus on diversity, under four key approaches: Chemistry for All, Chemistry for Scholars, Chemistry for Good and Chemistry for Community.
- STEM Learning offers CPD and enrichment for science teachers across the country, as well as a wealth of resources to download.
- The Association for Science Education (ASE) provides extensive resources for teachers and technicians in primary, secondary and post-16 settings.
- BBC Teach has a series of resources sorted into biology, chemistry and physics, providing lots of video clips to use in lessons.
- NASA provides videos and content focused on space education, sorted by educational phase in American schools (US Grades 6 to 12 match up to UK Years 7 to 13).

Further reading

Institute of Physics (2017) *Improving Gender Balance: Reflections on the Impact of Interventions in Schools.* Available at: https://www.iop.org/sites/default/files/2019-07/IGB-reflections-intervention.pdf

CHAPTER 12
HOW DO I TEACH CONTROVERSIAL TOPICS?

What do we mean by a 'controversial topic'?

There are a number of topics within the science National Curriculum that generate controversy. Crick (1998) defines a controversial topic as:

... an issue about which there is no one fixed or universally held point of view. Such issues are those which commonly divide society and for which significant groups offer conflicting explanations and solutions.

Why teach controversial topics?

Science teaching at secondary school involves dealing with topics, debates and ideas about which students have definite, strong and controversial opinions. It is important that science teachers are prepared to take on these topics, presenting evidence and showing students how to analyse it, and explaining with confidence why certain schools of thought are accepted by the wider scientific community.

The National Curriculum for science states:

Through building up a body of key foundational knowledge and concepts, pupils should be encouraged to recognise the power of rational explanation and develop a sense of excitement and curiosity about natural phenomena.

If we want students to recognise the 'power of rational explanation', we must explore specific areas where rational explanation can be used to draw conclusions. In Chapter 1, we stated that a reason for teaching science to students is so they can engage with major global challenges and become responsible and informed citizens who are capable of debating these topics. If this goal is to be achieved, these topics must be examined in the security of science classrooms. Controversial topics provide one of the best contexts for talking about the scientific method, by modelling how scientists think, how ideas form, and how evidence can be used to overturn scientific orthodoxy!

What common approaches can teachers use in science classrooms?

The fundamental principle underpinning the approach to teaching controversial topics should be one of science learning; students should be taught to engage with controversial topics *as scientists*. They should be directed to think scientifically about current issues, so it is essential they are given the chance to engage with these complex debates. For science teachers feeling nervous about where the debate might end up, reassurance is at hand; wherever the debate goes, it should remain firmly in the realm of learning to work scientifically.

You can structure this learning by your actions before, during and after teaching.

Before the lesson

Plan! Before the lesson, spend a few minutes predicting what controversial opinions or ideas students might come up with and practise your response – make a few brief notes or role play with a colleague if you are really nervous.

Remember to frame the topic as learning about science:

Today we are going to start looking at how diseases like HIV and AIDS are spread. This is a controversial topic in society, and people have lots of different perspectives and ideas. However, in our science lessons, we are going to focus on this topic as scientists would …

During the lesson

In teacher explanations, promote open-minded approaches:

As a scientist, it is important to be open minded. We are learning about stem cell research and there are lots of ethical considerations – should embryos be used to harvest stem cells, for example? You might have one idea about the answer to that question today, but as a scientist, the important thing is to always be open minded to new evidence. There might be new research tomorrow that changes your mind, and a good scientist would be open to that!

During the lesson, students are likely to ask a whole raft of questions. This can be one of the most high-stress parts of teaching controversial topics, as you can't plan for the unexpected questions. Again, the best strategy is always to bring the discussion back to scientific thinking, often by asking questions back to the student:

That's an interesting perspective. Thinking like a scientist, what evidence have you used to come to that conclusion?

Or:

Good point, that is a perspective we often see in the media or online. As scientists, let's talk for a moment about what makes a reliable scientific source. Does anyone know what peer review is? Before scientists can publish research, it is checked by other respected scientists in the field to make sure it is well done and reliable. A piece of research that has been peer reviewed is, therefore, the gold standard for scientists. Scientists generally get their information from peer-reviewed sources, rather than from the media which doesn't have the same standards.

The trickiest student 'question' of all can come in the form of a statement:

My dad says he smoked 30 cigarettes a day and it never did him any harm.

The same science-focused approach is the best reply:

That's a great example to help us talk about the difference between anecdotal evidence and a research study.

Consider this often-stated view:

My mum says that climate change is just exaggerated in the media. If climate change is real, why did it rain all summer?

You could reply:

Asking a question like that is a great way of thinking like a scientist. Scientists start their research by asking questions like 'why did it rain all summer?'. Then they have a look at all the evidence they can find – there's lots of reading in science! And they would start to find there's a difference between climate and weather.

The most controversial question of all might come as a follow up:

... are you saying my mum's wrong then?

To which there are a variety of answers:

Well, the evidence suggests ...

I'm saying that her perspective doesn't sound like a scientific perspective. The scientific perspective says ...

It's really important in a science classroom to be open minded to different ideas based on the best available evidence. The best available evidence I've seen suggests a different scientific answer to the one your mum has.

Can you remind me of the difference between opinion and a scientific theory? A scientific theory is the best possible explanation we have based on current evidence. We can all have different opinions, but what we are examining here is the most accurate theory we have access to.

After the lesson

Sometimes, the correct teacher response is 'I don't know, but I'll go and find out', a perfectly valid scientific reaction. You could ask students to do the same: 'Let's all research it before next lesson and see what we find.' When this happens, remember to make a note to look up the information you want to share and spend a few minutes sharing it in the following lesson. Make sure you point out that, in going away and researching the answer to an unknown question, you are thinking and working like a scientist.

What about religion in science?

In 1936, Albert Einstein wrote a letter to a sixth-grade student named Phyllis Wright answering the question 'do scientists pray?'. The letter was originally written in German and there are varying English translations that attempt to convey Einstein's nuanced and layered take on science, religion and the spirituality he found in studying the 'Laws of the Universe'.

January 24, 1936

Dear Phyllis,

I will attempt to reply to your question as simply as I can. Here is my answer:

Scientists believe that every occurrence, including the affairs of human beings, is due to the laws of nature. Therefore, a scientist cannot be inclined to believe that the course of events can be influenced by prayer, that is, by a supernaturally manifested wish.

However, we must concede that our actual knowledge of these forces is imperfect, so that in the end the belief in the existence of a final, ultimate spirit rests on a kind of faith. Such belief remains widespread even with the current achievements in science.

But also, everyone who is seriously involved in the pursuit of science becomes convinced that some spirit is manifest in the laws of the Universe, one that is vastly superior to that of man. In this way the pursuit of science leads to a religious feeling of a special sort, which is surely quite different from the religiosity of someone more naive.

With cordial greetings,

your A. Einstein

How *not* to teach controversial topics

If it is not science, it doesn't have a place in the science classroom. It is not appropriate for science teachers to introduce non-scientific perspectives into controversial debates. The role of the controversial topic is to teach students how scientists approach debate, not to explore sociological issues with varied perspectives.

But shouldn't we share all sides of the debate? No, not in the science classroom. The role of studying controversial topics in science is to enhance the scientific knowledge and skills of students. The emphasis should be on an open-minded, scientific process of discovery. An 'all-sides-of-the-argument' perspective is not required.

Controversial topics in practice

By looking at the National Curriculum, science teachers can identify topics in advance that might prove controversial. Knowing they are coming gives you the time and space to revise strategies to keep the lesson focused on science learning.

Subject and key stage	National Curriculum topic	Controversial questions	Potential misconceptions or alternative perspectives
Biology KS3	Reproduction in humans, including the structure and function of the male and female reproductive systems, menstrual cycle (without details of hormones), gametes, fertilisation, gestation and birth, to include the effect of maternal lifestyle on the fetus through the placenta	• Should people be allowed to use contraception? • Should abortion be allowed?	• 'My religion says that using contraception is a sin.' • 'Abortion is murder.' • 'It's a woman's right to choose.'
	The effects of recreational drugs (including substance misuse) on behaviour, health and life processes	• Should drugs be de-criminalised? • Should all drugs, including alcohol and tobacco, be banned?	• 'Smoking cannabis is harmless, in fact it's a good drug.' • 'Cannabis is natural so it must be good for you.' →

Subject and key stage	National Curriculum topic	Controversial questions	Potential misconceptions or alternative perspectives
Biology KS4	Health and disease: • Communicable diseases including sexually transmitted infections in humans (including HIV/AIDS) • The process of discovery and development of new medicines • The impact of lifestyle factors on the incidence of non-communicable diseases	• Should people be allowed to use barrier contraception? • Can we trust the drugs and medicine we are given? • Does what we do everyday affect our health?	• 'My religion says that abortion is wrong.' • 'I saw online that vaccines cause autism.' • 'My granddad smokes every day, and he is 95 and still healthy.'
Biology KS4	Evolution, inheritance and variation: • The potential impact of genomics on medicine • Sex determination in humans • The process of natural selection leading to evolution • The evidence for evolution	• Should we be allowed to edit people's DNA? • Should we be able to select traits in people? • Where does it stop, designer babies? • How does natural selection lead to changes in characteristics of a population? • What is the evidence for evolution?	• 'Yes, it will solve so many problems.' • 'I can't see it happening, so it can't be real.' • 'If we evolved from monkeys, why are there still monkeys?' • 'What if GM crops escape?' • 'I don't want to eat Frankenstein food.' →

Subject and key stage	National Curriculum topic	Controversial questions	Potential misconceptions or alternative perspectives
Biology KS4	• The importance of selective breeding of plants and animals in agriculture • The uses of modern biotechnology including gene technology; some of the practical and ethical considerations of modern biotechnology	• Should we selectively breed animals as it can lead to health issues (in certain breeds of dogs for instance)? • Should we genetically modify crops, animals or even people?	
Chemistry KS3	• Life cycle assessment and recycling to assess environmental impacts associated with all the stages of a product's life • The viability of recycling of certain materials • Carbon compounds, both as fuels and feedstock, and the competing demands for limited resources • Fractional distillation of crude oil and cracking to make more useful materials	• Should we recycle and, if so, how much? • Can we make it easier to recycle? • Is climate change real? • Does oil used for fuel lead to climate change? • Are alternatives to oil and gas viable (e.g. heat pumps and electric cars)? • Will crude oil run out? • Should the UK be more self-reliant for energy?	• 'Recycling is a waste of time; it all just goes to landfill anyway.' • 'Climate change isn't caused by humans. It's caused by the Sun.' • 'It's too expensive to replace boilers with heat pumps.' • 'It's a good thing to extract more oil and gas from the North Sea.'

→

Subject and key stage	National Curriculum topic	Controversial questions	Potential misconceptions or alternative perspectives
Chemistry KS4	Earth and atmospheric science: • Evidence for composition and evolution of the Earth's atmosphere since its formation • Evidence, and uncertainties in evidence, for additional anthropogenic causes of climate change • Potential effects of, and mitigation of, increased levels of carbon dioxide and methane on the Earth's climate • Common atmospheric pollutants: sulfur dioxide, oxides of nitrogen, particulates and their sources	• Are Ultra Low Emission Zones and low traffic neighbourhoods practical? • Is climate change caused by humans? • Is it climate change or weather?	• 'If the Earth's atmosphere is constantly changing, how do we know rises in carbon dioxide are caused by people?' • 'Climate change isn't real – it's summer and it's cold today.' • 'Climate change is caused by a hole in the ozone layer.' • 'General everyday pollution has nothing to do with climate change.' • 'I live in a city and I'm fine, the pollution can't be that bad.'

→

Subject and key stage	National Curriculum topic	Controversial questions	Potential misconceptions or alternative perspectives
Physics KS3	Radioactive materials, half-life, irradiation, contamination and their associated hazardous effects, waste disposal	• Should nuclear power be an option for power generation? • How do we safely store or dispose of nuclear waste?	• 'Nuclear power is bad, I don't want it near me.'

Further reading

Crick, B. (1998) *Education for Citizenship and the Teaching of Democracy in Schools.* Available at: https://dera.ioe.ac.uk/id/eprint/4385/1/crickreport1998.pdf

Dillon, J. (2009) 'Approaching soft disasters in the classroom: teaching about controversial issues in science, technology, society and environment education'. In, Jones, A. and de Vries, M. (Eds) *International Handbook of Research and Development in Technology Education.* (pp. 297–306). Leiden: Brill.

Oulton, C., Dillon, J. and Grace, M. (2004) 'Reconceptualising the teaching of controversial issues'. *International Journal of Science Education* 26 (4), 411–423.

Popova, M. (2013) 'Do Scientists Pray? Einstein Answers a Little Girl's Question about Science vs Religion', *The Marginalian.* Available at: https://www.themarginalian.org/2013/07/11/do-scientists-pray-einstein-letter-science-religion/

CHAPTER 13
WIDER READING TEXTS FOR SCIENCE TEACHERS

Setting reading as homework

There are 15 reading extracts on this list (one per term from Year 7 to Year 11). If you set one reading homework per term from the list below, by the end of Year 11, students will have had an enormously powerful science enrichment experience.

These extracts have been chosen because they are by an influential or respected author in the field, because they represent respected sources of scientific information (where you can 'read like a scientist'), because they expand student understanding of diversity in the field, or because they help teachers develop the disciplinary knowledge of their students – knowing what it means to be a scientist.

Supporting reading homework

To support reading homework, use these top tips:

1 Make sure you clearly tell students why the text has been chosen, who the author is and why the article has value in the science curriculum.

2 Set some simple questions to help students identify the key points in the text – think comprehension questions.

3 Before they attempt the homework, talk to students about the reading strategies required (see Chapter 10).

4 Start the following lesson with a quick discussion or recap of the article. Praise students for reading and engaging with a scientific text of value.

Eve Curie (1938) *Madame Curie*

A beautiful biography of Marie Curie, written in an accessible storytelling style that brings her struggles and successes to life vividly. In particular, see the sections on her physically draining but ultimately successful hunt for radium (pp. 170–178); the Curies visit to their workshop in the dark and finding it alive with softly glowing radium (p. 173); and the work Marie Curie did at the front in World War I setting up radiology equipment to x-ray wounded soldiers (pp. 287–288).

Atul Gawande (2007) *Better: A surgeon's notes on performance*

Lots of students have aspirations to work in medicine. The extract tells the story of Thomas, a strong, confident Afro-Caribbean man, who undergoes a surgery that puts him in long-term intensive care (pp. 154–157). The message is that, for surgeons, 'understanding their limits is the most difficult thing of all'.

Ewen Callaway (2023) 'Ancient DNA reveals the living descendants of enslaved people through 23andMe'

Nature, 03 August 2023. Available at: www.nature.com/articles/d41586-023-02478-9

A news article from *Nature*, reporting on a study using DNA analysis to find living descendants of African–Americans, free and enslaved, who had been buried in a site in Maryland in the 1700s.

John Hershey (1946) *Hiroshima*

A moving account of the reality on the ground after the atomic bomb was dropped on Hiroshima. It's only five chapters long, focused on the stories of a few survivors. Extracts describe the physical injuries of survivors (pp. 39–41), the journey of Mr Tanimoto across the ruins and past survivors in the immediate aftermath (pp. 60–61), and the work of scientists to measure the force of the bomb and then censor this information (pp. 106–108).

Richard Dawkins (2009) *The Greatest Show on Earth: The evidence for evolution*

This book is not an 'easy read'. The language is dense and scientific. However, short extracts scaffolded with good questions can make this text accessible to secondary school students, who will then get to read important ideas about evolution in the words of one of the most important scientists of the day. Extracts include a section on how scientists measure time in the thousands of millions of years (pp. 86–88) and some lovely explanations of the role senses play in natural selection of birds (pp. 54–56).

Ben Goldacre (2008) *Bad Science*

A fantastic book for exploring disciplinary science with students. Goldacre systematically shows how science done badly can have damaging real-world effects. Extracts include the difference between evidence and hypothesis in media reporting of science stories (pp. 237–241), the importance of blind trials (pp. 45–47) and statistics in science (pp. 256–258).

Michio Kaku (2011) *Physics of the Future: The inventions that will transform our lives*

This fascinating book explores research to describe future developments in many areas that are relevant to the curriculum. Possible extracts include sections on stem cells (p. 127), solar power (p. 215), nuclear fission (p. 219), many aspects of space travel (Chapter 6) and even whether we can resurrect dinosaurs (p. 161). However, I would be tempted to share 'A day in the life 2100' (pp. 353–356).

Mick O'Hare (ed.) (2014) *Question Everything: 132 science questions and their unexpected answers*

The questions in this book are from *New Scientist* magazine. Sharing an extract exposes students to that magazine, while reinforcing that science is an answers-seeking field of study. Chapters on Earth, space, biology, alcohol, physics, evolution and chemistry mean there is something for everyone.

Caroline Criado Perez (2019) *Invisible Women: Exposing data bias in a world designed for men*

Focused on exploring how women are systematically excluded in society, this is a good text for getting students thinking about data and statistics, and the way they are used in the real world. Good starting points are extracts on the way medical training focuses on the male body as the norm (pp. 196–198) and how women are at greater risk in pandemics (pp. 298–299).

Dara McAnulty (2020) *Diary of a Young Naturalist*

This book would be an outstanding text to share, both for its content celebrating nature and environmental activism, but also as a book written by a 17-year-old with autism, using his love of nature to cope with mental health issues, home moving and challenges at school. Extracts include some of his school experiences in the context of wanting to become a scientist (pp. 88–89) and a description of immersing himself in birdlife as an escape. He also describes his difficulties forming friendships and explores how interest in wildlife can be an escape from feeling different (p. 62).

Primo Levi (1975) *The Periodic Table*

In this text, Primo Levi combines memoirs of his family and life experiences (including his survival of Auschwitz) with his career in chemistry. The chapter 'Cerium' begins with a memory from Auschwitz, when his theft of some cerium alloy (from which cigarette lighters were made) helped save his life. This extract explores issues of inhumanity and the Holocaust, and connects them with chemistry through Levi's experience.

World Meteorological Organisation (2023) *State of the Global Climate 2022*

Available at: https://storymaps.arcgis.com/stories/6d9fcb0709f64904aee371eac09afbdf

An interactive online report, which sets out a variety of statistics about climate change impacts concerning atmosphere, land, cryosphere and ocean, while documenting extreme events. This provides an excellent opportunity to talk to students about the disciplinary skill of understanding statistics and how to analyse graphs.

Oliver Sacks (2001) *Uncle Tungsten*

Oliver Sacks might be the writer who writes most passionately about his love for science. In the chapter 'Uncle Tungsten', he reminisces about his childhood adoration of chemistry, and how he learned from his family and the world around him by reading and immersing himself in chemical experimentation and knowledge. The book is absolutely jammed with facts, insights and explorations of the history of chemistry, and almost any part would be worth sharing. Highlights include his childish love of metals and knowledge of their different properties (pp. 1–2) and his dawning awareness of the 'mysterious laws and phenomena' which underpin scientific inquiry (pp. 5–7).

Margot Lee Shetterly (2016) *Hidden Figures*

In *Hidden Figures*, Shetterly explores the previously unrecognised contribution to the space race of African–American women working in maths, physics and engineering. The extract has a great explanation of some of the physics calculations needed for a suborbital flight, and how Katherine Johnson became the first African–American woman to be a named author on a report by the Aerospace Mechanics Division (pp. 190–192).

Jim Al-Khalili (2010) *Pathfinders: the Golden Age of Arabic Science*

This book explores the pioneering science done by Arabic scientists and mathematicians in the Middle Ages, stories which are often underrepresented in Western classrooms. Extracts include the work of chemists Jābir and al-Rāzi on classification of materials (pp. 63–65), a section arguing that Snell's Law of optics should more accurately be attributed to Ibn Sahl, who was working on optics 650 years earlier (pp. 156–158) and biographies of al-Bīrūni and Ibn Sīna, whose name was latinised in Europe to Avicenna (pp. 175–177).

Using a reading text in practice

Primo Levi, the author and narrator, was an Italian–Jewish chemist. In 1944, he was sent to Auschwitz by the Nazis and survived almost a year there, until its liberation in 1945. After the war, he wrote books about his experience. The suggested extract is taken from *The Periodic Table*. In 2006, The Royal Institution voted this the best science book ever written. In the book, Levi writes about elements and how they are connected to his life story.

Here is an example of how the suggested extract by Primo Levi could be used either for homework or in class.

Pre-reading questions

Discuss these questions *before* students tackle the reading exercise. This discussion establishes some prior knowledge that will scaffold students to effectively access the text.

1 What do you know about Auschwitz? What do you know about work and punishments in Auschwitz?

Recap the role of Auschwitz in Poland as a group of concentration and extermination camps in the Holocaust in the Second World War. Students may not be aware that some prisoners worked in different slave labour roles in the camps. Sometimes, working in these 'jobs' gave prisoners access to food or supplies that – if stolen – could help to keep them alive. But the punishment for being caught was death.

2 If the punishment for theft was death, why do you think prisoners would have risked stealing?

Draw attention to the intense need for food that prisoners experienced.

3 The extract is entitled 'Cerium'. Predict what we *might* learn about the element in this extract.

What would you like to learn from reading this extract?

'Cerium'

According to Alberto, the price of a lighter flint was equivalent to a ration of bread, that is, one day of life; I had stolen at least 40 rods, from each of which could be **obtained** three finished flints. The total: 120 flints, two months of life for me and two for Alberto, and in two months the Russians would have arrived and liberated us; and finally the cerium would have **liberated** us, an element about which I knew nothing, save for that single practical application, and that it belongs to the equivocal and heretical **rare earth group** family, and that its name has nothing to do with the Latin and Italian word for wax (cera) and it was not named after its discoverer; instead it celebrates (great modesty of the chemists of past times!) the **asteroid** Ceres, since the metal and the star were discovered in the same year, 1801; and this was perhaps an affectionate-ironic homage to alchemical couplings: just as the sun was gold and Mars iron, so Ceres must be cerium.

> What do Primo Levi and Alberto plan to swap the lighter flints for?

> List three things we learn about the element cerium.

That evening I brought into camp the small rods and Alberto a metal plate with a round hole: it was the prescribed **calibre** to which we had to thin down the rods in order to transform them into flints and therefore bread.

What then occurred should be judged with caution. Alberto said the rods must be reduced by scraping them with a knife, on the sly, so that no competitor could steal our secret. When? At night. Where? In the wooden hut, under the blankets and on top of the pallet full of shavings – thus running the risk of starting a fire and more realistically, being hanged: for this was the punishment meted out, among other transgressions, to all those who lit a match in the hut.

> What are the two risks the men face while scraping the cerium to make flints?

…

While our companions slept, we worked with a knife, night after night. The scene was so sad you could weep: a single electric light bulb weakly lit the large wooden hut, and in the shadows, as in a vast cave, the faces of other men were visible, wracked by sleep and dreams: tinged with death, they worked their jaws furiously, dreaming of eating. Many of them had an arm or a naked skeletal foot hanging over the side of the bunk, others moaned or talked in their sleep.

> What details tell the reader that the prisoners in Auschwitz are starving?

But we two were alive and did not give way to sleep. We kept the blanket raised with our knees and beneath that **improved** tent scraped away at the small rods, blindly and by touch: at each stroke you heard a slight crackle and saw a spray of yellow sparks spurt up. At intervals we tested to see if the rod passed through the sample hold: if it didn't, we continued to scrape; if it did, we broke off the thinned-down stub and set it carefully aside.

Why do you think they have to scrape the rods 'blindly and by touch'?

We worked for three nights: nothing happened, nobody noticed our activity, nor did the blanket or pallet catch fire, and this is how we won the bread which kept us alive until the arrival of the Russians and how we comforted each other in the trust and friendship which united us. What happened to me is described elsewhere. Alberto left on foot with the majority of the prisoners when the front drew near: the Germans made them walk for days and nights in snow and freezing cold, slaughtering all those who could not go on: and then they loaded them onto open freight cars, which transported the few survivors to a new chapter of slavery, Buchenwald and Mauthausen. No more than a fourth of those who left survived the march.

In what two ways did making the flints help Primo Levi and Alberto?

What do you think Primo Levi's message about survival in Auschwitz seems to be?

Alberto did not return and not a trace remains of him.

What happened to Alberto?

Vocabulary development

Reading a literary extract is a powerful opportunity to develop and reinforce student literacy.

Tier 2 words

Highlight some Tier 2 words, such as those shown in bold in the extract. Encourage students to try out using these words. Remember, Tier 2 words are valuable academic words that are useful in subjects across the curriculum (pages 22–3).

Create a bank of Tier 2 words, and reward students who use them in their own writing, for example:

- improvise/improvised
- obtain/obtained
- liberate/liberated
- judge/judged.

Tier 3 words

Tier 3 words (pages 22–3) are the science-specific words that students have to recognise in order to understand the text:

- element
- rare earth group
- asteroid
- calibre.

Explain these words before the exercise, perhaps by providing a glossary. You could also ask students to write a summary of their learning using these words after the exercise.

Post-reading questions

You could use these questions to structure discussion after reading. Ask students to choose the answer they most agree with – use finger-voting. Cold call students, asking them to explain their answer.

Some answers test factual understanding and there is a clear right answer, given at the end. For open questions, bounce the discussion to students who have chosen different answers by asking them to 'add to or challenge the previous speaker'.

1   What does Levi say bread was worth in Auschwitz?

   A   An hour of life

   B   A day of life

   C   A week of life

   D   A month of life

2   What did you learn about the element cerium?

   A   It can be traded for food and it was named after the asteroid Ceres

   B   It can be used to make lighter flints and it was named after the asteroid Ceres

   C   It can be used to make lighter flints and it was named after its discoverer

3   How did Primo and Alberto change the cerium rods into lighter flints?

   A They scraped them with a knife until they were the right size

   B They collected them together and worked on them at night

   C They cut them up by looking closely at them to check the size

   D They scraped them with a knife, testing they were the right standard size using a metal plate with a round hole

4   What positives did Primo and Alberto get from stealing the cerium?

   A Bread, trust and friendship

   B Money, safety and friendship

   C Bread, trust and survival

5   What happened to Alberto?

   A He died in Auschwitz

   B He was forced to go on a brutal walk in extreme conditions to another camp and died somewhere on the journey

   C He survived the war but no one knows where he is

6   What do you think Primo Levi's message about survival in Auschwitz seems to be?

   A Survival was simply down to luck or chance

   B Survival was the result of working together and helping each other

   C Survival required prisoners to take big risks

   D Survival was impossible

   E Survival was impossible to control

Answers

1   B

2   B

3   D (A is also correct, but D is more precise)

4   A (A is the only answer explicitly referenced in the text)

5   B (students are required to infer his death)

6   A, B, C and E can all be argued but D is wrong as Levi himself survived